44
COUNTRY
TRAILS

Canadian Cataloguing in Publication Data

Jacob, Katherine, 1967-
    44 country trails: The Conservation Lands of Ontario

Includes bibliographical references and index.

Copyright © 1998 Katherine Jacob

ISBN 0-9683425-0-7

1. Trails – Ontario, Southern – Guidebooks. 2. Hiking – Ontario, Southern –
Guidebooks. 3. Natural areas – Ontario, Southern – Guidebooks. 4. Ontario,
Southern – Guidebooks. I. The Conservation Lands of Ontario (Association).
II. Title. III. Title: 44 Country Trails.

FC3095.S67J32 1998   917.1304'4   C98-930655-0
F1059.S67J32 1998

Printed by Ampersand Printing, Guelph, Ontario

This book is for information purposes only, and the author and publisher take no
responsibility for, nor guarantee, the accuracy of all the information contained in the
book. Trail conditions may change, vary and be re-routed over time. Man-made
obstacles, obstructions, alterations or new construction on or near the trails may also
change or affect conditions as described in this book. The author and publisher cannot
be held responsible for any thefts, problems, injuries or misfortunes that occur from
use of the material in this book. Remember that SAFETY is a personal responsibility.

Author: Katherine Jacob
Editors: Jim Reid, Joan Bell
Cartography by: Paul Heersink, Paperglyphs Cartographic Services
Front Cover Photo: Hilton Falls Conservation Area, Halton Region
                     Conservation Authority.

First Printing, April 1998 - 5000
    Reprint, August 1998 - 5000
    Reprint, March 2000 - 5000

Maps produced by The Conservation Lands of Ontario with permission from the:
    Grand River, Halton Region, Hamilton Region, Long Point Region, and
    Niagara Peninsula Conservation Authorities, Ontario Ministry of Natural
    Resources. Copyright, Queen's Printer, 1998, and Elora Cataract Trailway
    Association, Copyright, 1996.

44
COUNTRY
TRAILS

THE CONSERVATION LANDS OF ONTARIO

by KATHERINE JACOB

 Grand River Conservation Authority

 Halton Region Conservation Authority

 Hamilton Region Conservation Authority

 Niagara Peninsula Conservation Authority

 Long Point Region Conservation Authority

This is the first guide published by The Conservation Lands of Ontario an environmental and business alliance focusing on adventure and eco-tourism in watersheds managed by the following Conservation authorities:

Grand River Conservation Authority

Halton Region Conservation Authority

Hamilton Region Conservation Authority

Niagara Peninsula Conservation Authority

Long Point Region Conservation Authority

The Conservation Lands of Ontario
400 Clyde Rd., P.O. Box 729
Cambridge, Ontario
N1R 5W6
1-888-376-2212
conservationlands@grandriver.on.ca

This project has been financially assisted by the Ontario Government's Niagara Escarpment Program through the Ontario Heritage Foundation and the Canadian Tourism Commission

We acknowledge and thank the Canadian Automobile Association for its generous financial contribution and continued participation as a Conservation Lands Partner and Sponsor of the First Edition of *44 Country Trails*.

This book is dedicated to my Mom,
whose afternoon meadow walks and forest picnics inspired
my love and exploration of nature at an early age.
Your support to this day has enriched my life.

A SPECIAL THANKS TO ALL MY friends and family
who walked these trails with me and provided support, encouragement
and ideas; especially Renate for inspiration; Carol for believing; Laszlo
for planting the idea; Joe for editing; Leanne and Todd for proofing;
Mom, Mary, Leanne, Aaron, Amber & Blayne, Pete and Joe for walking;
Bernie & Ali, Craig & Laurie, Mike & Mary, Jim, Marian, Bob, John for
support, advice and ideas; Sherri, Barb, Jen, Genevieve, Sue, Wayne,
Leanne & Richard, Todd, Marilyn, Eric for encouragement; Ralph, Jim,
Joan, David, Christine, Marjorie, Janice, Gary, Marg and all staff at the
Conservation Authorities for time, energy and assistance. And to Dad
and Scott, whose spirits, I know, were with me during this project.

TABLE OF CONTENTS

INTRODUCTION

It is a treasure, within such a densely populated region of Ontario, to have natural areas to which we can escape. Dense woodlands are fringed with ferns, paths wind around limestone outcrops and tumbling rapids enliven waterways. In the spring, wildflowers adorn the forest floor, bright yellow marsh marigolds colour wetlands and deer browse along river banks. In the fall, green leaves unfold into autumn hues, parachuting poplar seeds dance in the breeze and kettles of broad-winged hawks soar above curtains of red and gold.

Cascading waterfalls, towering rock faces and birds calling from forest canopies are among the wonders that enclose southern Ontario's country trails. The Conservation Lands of Ontario embraces several world-class natural areas – two World Biosphere Reserves, a Canadian Heritage River and the rare Carolinian forest zone.

The designation of a world biosphere reserve is granted by the United Nations Educational, Scientific and Cultural Organization (UNESCO) to conserve significant ecological features of an area.

The Niagara Escarpment World Biosphere Reserve stretches 782 kilometres (486 miles) from Niagara to Tobermory. More than 430 million years ago, the escarpment, in the shape of a gigantic horseshoe, was the rim of a warm, shallow sea. The escarpment's limestone cliffs, covering a vast area from Ontario to Michigan, emerged when the sea withdrew and the great ice sheets melted. Ancient, twisted eastern white cedars that cling to these cliffs are more than 1,500 years old.

The Long Point World Biosphere Reserve has one of the longest freshwater sand spits in the world. At 40 kilometres (24.9 miles), the undisturbed sand dunes, woodlands, shallow bays and extensive marsh system of Long Point's Inner Bay is a major staging area for migrating waterfowl, shorebirds and songbirds.

The Grand River flows south from Georgian Bay for 298 kilometres (185 miles) to its mouth at Lake Erie. It is the first river situated in a densely populated region of Canada to receive a Canadian Heritage River designation. Known internationally for one of the best brown trout fisheries in North America, the river's beauty and accessibility also lure hikers, canoeists and kayakers.

Each of these areas enfold the rare Carolinian Forest, a temperate zone that contains plants and animals typically found farther south in the United States. You won't find the sassafras, tulip and cucumber magnolia trees, or the cerulean warbler, spiny softshell turtle and wild indigo duskywing butterfly elsewhere in Canada.

Although these natural areas have diverse habitats, one common feature they share are plant communities and wildlife populations that are provincially and nationally rare. Regrettably, as development in Ontario spreads, these plant communities and animal populations decline due to human impact and loss of habitat. In the face of these changes, the preservation activities of the Conservation Authorities are of great importance.

These community-based environmental agencies restore, develop and manage natural resources within a watershed, a land region drained by a river or stream and its tributaries. Also noteworthy are their activities in flood management, habitat protection, ecosystem regeneration and outdoor recreation. Conservation Authorities provide an extensive trail system so we can experience these unique and fragile natural areas.

The trails in this book are in the watersheds of the Grand River, Halton Region, Hamilton Region, Niagara Peninsula, and Long Point Region Conservation Authorities.

These trails will take you to special natural features that are historically and environmentally significant. It is my hope that as you enjoy these trails, you will understand the need to conserve these vulnerable lands. Nature trails are living connections between humans and wildlife that cannot be taken for granted.

Enjoy the Trails!

Katherine

HOW TO USE THIS GUIDE

This guide offers brief descriptions and detailed maps for each trail. At the start of each description, the distance is mentioned. A loop trail means a return to the starting point via another route. If linear, the trail returns to the starting point via the same route. Some trails have parking lots at starting and end points and other access locations allowing for the arrangement of a car shuttle.

Many conservation areas have other trails on their properties and some of these trails connect with the main trail. These are listed in brackets as "Other Area Trails".

Many of these trails connect with major trail links such as the Bruce Trail, Waterfront Trail and the Trans Canada Trail. Other Conservation Area trails are close to one another and can easily be combined into a day or weekend trip.

Major trail links are briefly described and highlighted on the fold-out map, but consult individual trail guides for detailed information (addresses and phone numbers are provided). The Bruce Trail is the most common link and is shown on the trail maps as a point of reference.

Symbols for trail features and facilities appear on the individual Trail Maps. The matrix in the back section lists permitted uses. Only a few trails offer track-set skiing, but snowshoes can be used in winter on most walking trails. The special features listing indicates unique trail information such as special events and interpretive centres. It also indicates other seasonal conservation area and trail uses, such as snowmobiling and hunting. If a conservation area allows hunting, call before visiting in the spring and fall.

A phone number for more information on a specific trail is listed, only if it differs from the conservation authority's main telephone number. Please call during the off-season to ensure the conservation area is open. If it is closed, hiking is often permitted, but facilities won't be available.

Environmental Ethics

Since these trails are primarily for the enjoyment of nature, there are environmental ethics to observe. Widening a trail by foot can alter the habitat and some plants take years to grow back. Consequently, proceed directly through wet, muddy spots. Don't litter, or trample vegetation around the edges of a trail. And don't deliberately make noise to spook animals; they need their energy to search for food.

As adventurous as they may look, side trails should be avoided as vegetation may be harmed. Stay on marked trails and within lookout area boundaries to help protect the rare plants and fragile natural resources, as well as for your own safety.

Pets must be kept on a leash. Dogs can chase wildlife, harm ground-nesting songbirds and transfer poison ivy to owners.

Safety Notes

On a cautionary note, there are inherent risks in travelling on foot through natural areas. On escarpment properties, many trails edge the escarpment and there aren't fences to guard against steep slopes. Some crevices, starting right at the edge of the trail, are hidden by pine trees and bushes. Depending on weather and time of the year, some trail surfaces near the water can be muddy or icy. Limestone can also be dangerous and slippery when wet.

Poison ivy takes many forms and is quite rampant off the maintained trail areas. Look for three shiny leaflets on a single stem with the middle leaf having a longer stalk.

Some trails are in remote locations. Lock all valuables in the trunk of your car to ensure the safety of your belongings.

Trail Etiquette

Referred to as "multi-use trails," many paths might be shared by hikers, mountain bikers, equestrians and joggers. Here are some trail etiquette guidelines:

- Stay to the right and allow other users room to pass on your left. For example, joggers and cyclists should avoid travelling in 'packs.'
- Yield to pedestrians; they have the right of way on multi-use trails.

- When passing others, sound your bell (if on a bike) or call out ("On your left") and then pass safely on the user's left side. Be especially cautious when approaching horseback riders, children or dogs from behind.

- Say "Hi" when passing or approaching horseback riders, especially when on a bike. Horses have a large peripheral vision and may not perceive you as a human when you're on a bicycle. They are nervous animals and their first instinct will be to run. When approaching horseback riders, let them pass unless the rider indicates otherwise. If approaching from behind, slow to their speed and from 15 metres (49 feet) away ask if it is safe to pass slowly.

- Ride slowly down hills, under and across bridges and where trails curve sharply. Reduce your speed when the trail is busy or when your visibility is limited.

- Watch for surface hazards like broken glass, gravel and potholes. When cycling, cross railway tracks at a right angle to avoid getting your front wheel caught.

- Don't snowshoe over groomed ski trails. It breaks up the tracks for skiers.

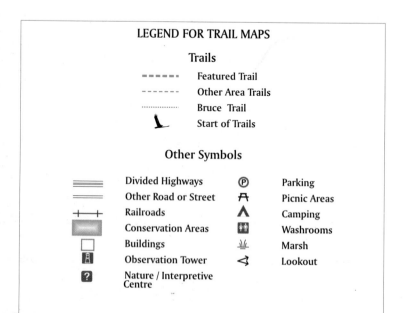

LEGEND FOR TRAIL MAPS

Trails

------	Featured Trail
------	Other Area Trails
....	Bruce Trail
⬇	Start of Trails

Other Symbols

≡	Divided Highways	Ⓟ	Parking
═	Other Road or Street	⛗	Picnic Areas
┼──┼	Railroads	⋀	Camping
▓	Conservation Areas	⛨	Washrooms
▢	Buildings	⩊	Marsh
▣	Observation Tower	⊲	Lookout
▣	Nature / Interpretive Centre		

Trans Canada Trail

Ontario trails make up about 25% of the total length of the 15,000-kilometre (9,320 mile) Trans Canada Trail (TCT), Canada's coast-to-coast trail system.

Many of the trails in this book will be linked to other community shared-use trails to create 3,000 kilometres (1,864 miles) of connecting Ontario trails which will form a portion of the Trans Canada Trail by the year 2000.

The 11-kilometre (6.8-mile) Caledon Trail Link, for example, connects Inglewood on the Caledon Trailway to the Forks of the Credit Provincial Park on the Elora Cataract Trailway. The Hamilton to Brantford Rail Trail and the Cambridge to Paris Rail Trail are also major connecting links in this trail system.

Trans Canada Trail Foundation
43 Westminster Ave. N.
Montreal West, Quebec
H4X 1Y8
(800) 465-3636
e-mail: info@tctrail.ca
website: www.tctrail.ca

Ontario Trails Council
Box 462, Stn. D.
Etobicoke, Ontario
M9A 4X4

The Bruce Trail

The Bruce Trail, Canada's oldest, long-distance trail, follows the Niagara Escarpment Biosphere Reserve through the most densely populated area of Canada before reaching the remote regions of Georgian Bay.

The trail stretches 782 kilometres (486 mi.) from Niagara to Tobermory, leading to 30-metre (100-foot) limestone cliffs, cascading waterfalls and crevice caves and passing mill ruins, old homesteads and abandoned farmland.

Most fascinating are ancient, twisted eastern white cedars, clinging to cliff faces. These weathered trees, some more than 1,500 years old, are part of a rare, pre-settlement forest which stretches across eastern North America.

The Bruce Trail Association
PO Box 857
Hamilton, Ontario
L8N 3N9
905-529-6821, 1-800-665-4453, fax 905-529-6823

Grand Valley Trail

The Grand Valley Trail stretches for 250 kilometres (155 miles) from Rock Point Provincial Park on Lake Erie to the town of Alton near Orangeville, Ontario. Much of the trail follows the Grand River with many boardwalk, log bridge and stream crossings. It passes along cornfields, through old farm orchards and forests.

Look for notable sights such as the Bell Homestead, home of Alexander Graham Bell; the Kissing Bridge at West Montrose, the only covered bridge still standing in Ontario; and Doon Heritage Crossroads, a living history museum on the outskirts of Kitchener-Waterloo.

Grand Valley Trail Association
75 King St. S.
P.O. Box 40068
RPO Waterloo Square
Waterloo, Ontario
N2J 4V1

Waterfront Trail

The Lake Ontario Waterfront Trail stretches 325 kilometres (202 miles) along the lake between Trenton and Niagara-on-the-Lake.

From Bronte Creek Provincial Park in Oakville, Van Wagners Ponds in Hamilton to Burlington's Brant Museum, the trail links natural areas, parks and promenades, marinas, yacht clubs, historic sites and museums. It also connects a system of inter-regional trails, such as the Ganaraska Trail and the Bruce Trail.

Waterfront Regeneration Trust
207 Queen's Quay West, Ste. 580
Toronto, Ontario
M5J 1A2
tel. (416) 314-8572
fax (416) 314-9497
e-mail: info@wrtrust.com
website: www.waterfronttrail.org

Niagara Parks Recreation Trail

The Niagara River Recreation Trail runs parallel to the Niagara River, stretching for 56 kilometres (35 miles) from Niagara-On-The-Lake to historic Fort Erie. Located along the Niagara River Parkway, it has easy access points, allowing shorter trips for those travelling with children. Along the trail, historical plaques, scenic resting spots and river views are found.

Designated as an important Bird Area by the Canadian Nature Federation, National Audubon Society and the American Bird Conservancy in the U.S., the Niagara River is one of the world's best gull-watching sites. Following the river and providing shore accessibility, the trail offers ideal vantage points to watch these birds during the fall and winter.

The Niagara Parks Commission
P.O. Box 150
Niagara Falls, Ontario
L2E 6T2
tel (905) 356-2241
fax (905) 354-6041
e-mail:npinfo@vaxxine.com
website: www.niagaraparks.com

APPS' MILL NATURE TRAIL

LOCATION: Apps' Mill Conservation Area, Brantford
DISTANCE: 3.6 km/2.2 mi. linear
RATING: Beginner
HIGHLIGHT: 1846 wooden flour and grist mill

TRAIL SURFACE:
Gravel from the nature centre to the mill; hard-packed earth with rocks and grass upstream of the mill.

DIRECTIONS: From Hwy. 401, take the Hwy. 24 South exit. Continue on Hwy. 75/24A through Paris, and take Hwy. 2 towards Woodstock. Turn left on Rest Acres Road and right on Robinson Road. Follow signs for the Apps' Mill Conservation area. From Hwy. 403, turn south at Rest Acres Road exit and turn right on Robinson Rd.

SPECIAL FEATURES: Nature centre.

MORE INFORMATION: (519) 752-0655.

This trail takes a step back in time as you walk along a former mill race leading to a wooden flour and grist mill built in 1846. One of the first to export wheat overseas, the Apps' Mill now stands inoperable, its millpond overgrown with cattails and jewelweed. The trail continues along a dike that used to hold back water for the mill pond.

The main path follows the floodplain of Whiteman's Creek. This cold water stream, home to brook, brown and rainbow trout, attracts fishermen to its banks. Other highlights are a visible spring that feeds the creek; the queen snake, a rare water reptile; and part of an old dam that extends midway into the creek.

Among the Russian olive, cottonwood and dogwood trees, are old beech and maple that survived the logging era of the 1920s. In the spring, side trails lead deeper into the forest where dark red trilliums sit next to bright yellow trout lilies, pockets of bloodroot are tucked into tree roots and mayapples uncurl like partially opened umbrellas. The main trail eventually leads onto the Cleaver Side Road to continue through Whiteman's Creek Angler Parking along the higher banks of the creek.

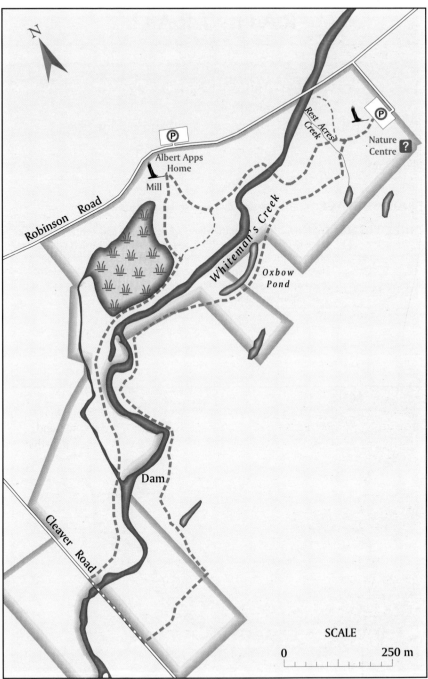

N

Robinson Road

P

Albert Apps
Home

Mill

Whiteman's Creek

Rest Acres Creek

P

Nature
Centre

?

Oxbow
Pond

Dam

Cleaver Road

SCALE

0   250 m

Copyright © The Conservation Lands of Ontario, 1998

CAMBRIDGE TO PARIS
RAIL TRAIL

DISTANCE: 19 km/11.8 mi. linear
RATING: Beginner
HIGHLIGHT: Follows a Canadian Heritage River

TRAIL SURFACE: Crushed gravel with some hard-packed earth.

DIRECTIONS: From Hwy. 401, take the Hwy. 24 South exit and continue through the city of Cambridge. The parking lot next to the GTO gas bar is on the right-hand side. For the Paris parking lot, continue on Hwy. 24 and turn right on East River Road through Glen Morris into Paris. As you enter the town, you'll see the parking lot on your right-hand side.

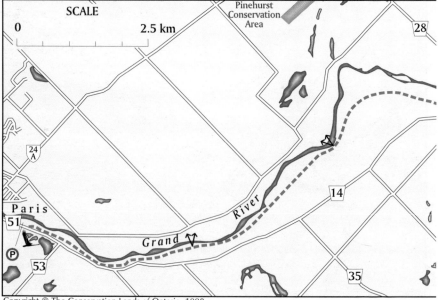

Copyright © The Conservation Lands of Ontario, 1998

There are few places in Canada where hikers can meander along a Canadian Heritage River and southern Ontario is fortunate to have one.

The Cambridge to Paris Rail Trail, formerly an electric railway line for the Lake Erie and Northern Railway, follows the Grand River along its eastern bank, offering spectacular views of the river, with benches and scenic overlooks.

There are a variety of wildflowers, the ruins of an old stone mill and a natural spring where people often stop to fill water bottles. Bring along binoculars to catch a glimpse of a wild turkey, red-bellied woodpecker or osprey. Travelling through the Carolinian forest zone, you may hear the explosive call of the cerulean warbler, or recognize unique tree and plant species such as hill's oak, large yellow lady's slippers and pignut hickory.

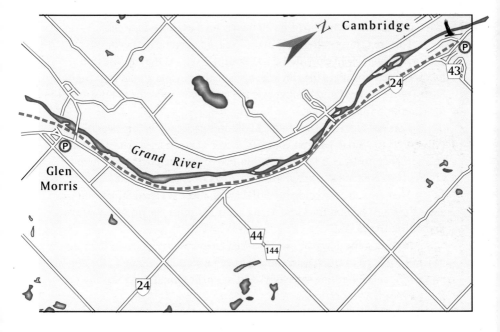

ELORA GORGE TRAIL

LOCATION:	Elora Gorge Conservation Area, Elora
DISTANCE:	2.5 km/1.5 mi. loop
RATING:	Beginner
HIGHLIGHT:	Gorge with 20-metre (65-foot) limestone cliffs
LINK:	Grand Valley Trail

TRAIL SURFACE: Hard-packed earth, pavement.

DIRECTIONS: From Hwy 401, take Hwy. 6 North towards Guelph. Turn left on Wellington Cty. Rd. 7 to Elora, left on Wellington Cty Rd. 21 and follow signs to the conservation area.

MORE INFORMATION: (519) 846-9742. Admission fee applies.

Formed by glacial meltwaters, the gorge runs for two kilometres (1.2 miles) through most of the conservation area's interior, offering spectacular lookout points from the top of its 20-metre (65-foot) limestone cliffs.

This trail starts at the Hole in the Wall, an opening in the limestone cliffs where stairs lead close to the fast-flowing river. At the top, the trail follows a footpath along the cliff edge, eventually passing an old ruin behind Little Folks Furniture and leading over the footbridge onto the main street in the charming village of Elora.

Note the Elora Mill, an 1800s five-storey grist mill, before heading up Price Street to a small park on your left. Lover's Leap, a legendary spot where an aboriginal princess is said to have jumped to her death when she found out her beloved had been killed in battle, marks a gorge overlook.

After crossing the bridge over the Irvine River at David Street, you enter the forest behind the Elora Arena and pass under the bridge to return to the Hole in the Wall.

In winter, the gorge has well-marked cross-country ski trails offering views of cedar trees laden with snow, a frozen waterfall clinging to the 20-metre (65-foot) limestone cliffs and sections of the Grand River flowing freely beneath layers of ice.

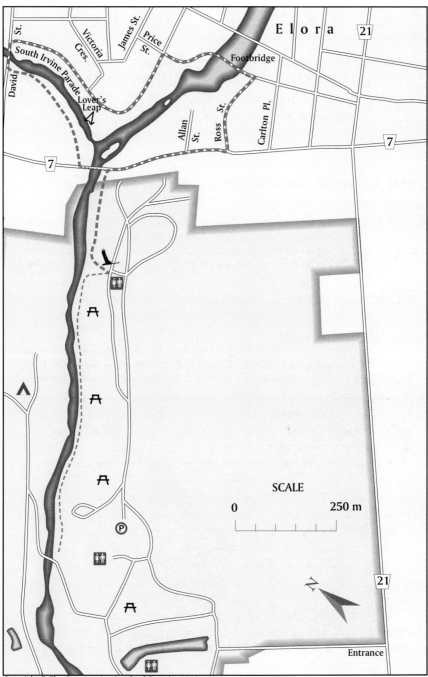

Copyright © The Conservation Lands of Ontario, 1998

THE ELORA
CATARACT TRAILWAY

DISTANCE:	47 km/29 mi. linear
RATING:	Beginner
HIGHLIGHT:	Swim at Elora Quarry
LINK:	Grand Valley Trail, Bruce Trail

TRAIL SURFACE: Stone dust, pavement, gravel, hard-packed earth with rocks and grass.

DIRECTIONS: From Hwy 401, take Hwy. 6 North towards Guelph. Turn left on Wellington Cty. Rd. 7 and follow it into the village of Elora. Turn right on Mill St. E. and left on Gerrie Road. To reach Forks of the Credit from the 401, take Hwy. 25 North, turn right on Hwy. 24, follow through Erin and turn right on Cataract Rd.

SPECIAL FEATURES: Snowmobiling access from Belwood Lake Conservation Area to the village of Erin.

MORE INFORMATION:
Elora Cataract Trailway Association, Box 99, Fergus, ON N1M 2W7 (519) 843-3650, fax (519) 843-6907. Admission fee applies if you stop over or use the facilities at Belwood Lake Conservation Area.

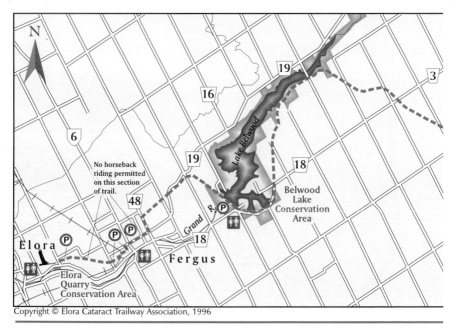

22

Starting on the outskirts of Elora, this trail meanders through the historic town of Fergus and continues past rolling hills, farmland and horses grazing in open fields.

Skirting the edge of the 12-kilometre (7.5-mile) Belwood Lake, climbing the hills of Erin and finishing at the Forks of the Credit Provincial Park, this former rail corridor links communities from Elora to Cataract. Families with baby carriages or tricycles; teens cycling from one community to the next; and people riding horses or walking their dogs mingle along the way.

The trail winds through peaceful rural settings and colourful wildflower meadows where butterflies dart to and fro. It also leads through lush forested areas offering welcome shade on a hot afternoon.

Once the trail leaves Belwood Lake's cottage area, the stone dust ends but the pathway is well defined.

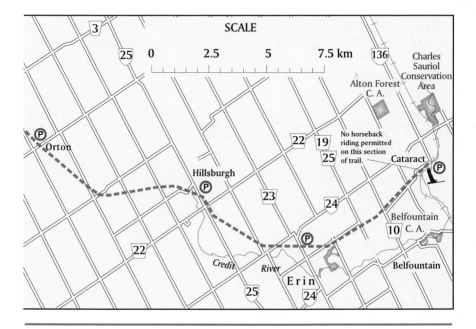

F.W.R. DICKSON TRAIL

LOCATION:	F.W.R. Dickson Wilderness Area, Cambridge
DISTANCE:	3.3 km/2.1 mi. linear (2 km/1.2 mi. loop in F.W.R. Dickson)
RATING:	Beginner
HIGHLIGHT:	Observation tower for migrating birds

TRAIL SURFACE: Hard-packed earth.

DIRECTIONS: From Hwy. 401, take the Hwy. 24 South exit into Cambridge. Continue on Hwy. 24A/Regional Rd. 75 south towards Paris. After you pass Waterloo Regional Rd. 49, you'll see a sign for Brant-Waterloo Rd. and Camp Ganadoweh on your right. Turn right onto this road, pass Hillside Lake Park and continue on a gravel road around a few winding turns. There's a parking lot for F.W.R. Dickson Wilderness Area on your right. To reach Bannister Lake, turn right on Waterloo Regional Rd. 49.

MORE INFORMATION: (519) 846-9742. Admission fee applies.

At F.W.R. Dickson Wilderness Area, chickadees feed from your hand, ducks swim in the pond and frogs serenade in the swamp. The main trail winds through a hardwood forest and crosses a swamp on two boardwalk sections. At the pond, stop to find the rare Pipsissewa flower along the banks or cross the bridge to walk around the outer edge of the pond bordering a tall grass prairie.

The walk around the south end of Wrigley Lake leads through a forest with a large variety of oak species. Black, northern pin, bur, white and red oaks border the trail.

If you cross Regional Road 49 into the parking lot near Bannister Lake, walk through a meadow path that leads to a large observation tower overlooking the lake. This is a prime spot to view migrating waterfowl such as green-winged teal, blue-winged teal and pintail ducks.

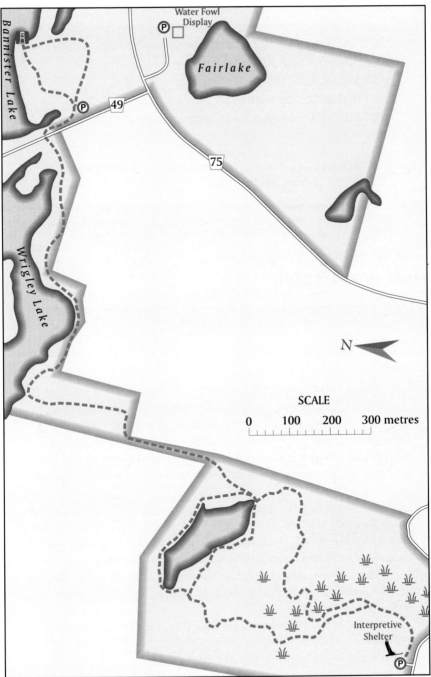

Water Fowl
Display

P

Fairlake

P 49

75

Bannister Lake

Wrigley Lake

N

SCALE

0   100   200   300 metres

Interpretive
Shelter

P

LUTHER MARSH TRAIL

LOCATION: Luther Marsh Conservation Area, north of Orangeville
DISTANCE: 7 km/4.3 mi. linear
RATING: Beginner
HIGHLIGHT: Migratory waterfowl, observation tower

TRAIL SURFACE: Gravel interior roads and grassed trails currently under development.

DIRECTIONS: From Hwy. 401, take Hwy. 25 north through Grand Valley. Turn west onto East Luther Township Sideroad 6-7. Follow this sideroad until it ends, then turn right and follow the signs to Luther.

SPECIAL FEATURES: Hunting season.

MORE INFORMATION:

(519) 928-2832. Admission fee applies. Bring insect repellent and drinking water. Hunting occurs from September to February on Monday, Wednesday, Friday and Saturday.

Luther Marsh is one of the largest inland marshes in the province and an important migration stopover for shorebirds. Herons wade along the edges of the marsh waiting to spear fish, osprey dive into the water with talons outstretched, and Wilson's phalarope dash to and fro in search of insects. Luther Marsh is a summer breeding ground for these species as well as provincially rare nesting birds such as the redhead, least bittern and great egret.

One of the largest wildlife and wetland areas in southern Ontario, you can explore Luther Marsh by its interior road system. Pause at observation towers for a better view. Aside from birds, provincially rare reptiles such as the spotted turtle and Butler's garter snake can also be spotted.

The site is dominated by Luther Lake, a 4,000-hectare (9,884-acre) shallow, marshy lake containing several islands and surrounded by an extensive, low-shrub bog.

Luther Marsh has four wetland types (bog, marsh, swamp and fen meadows) normally not found in one area. In fact, Wylde Lake bog is the largest undisturbed bog in southern Ontario.

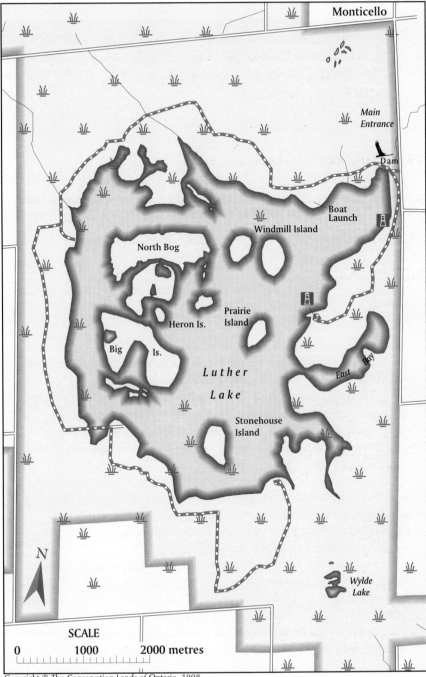

Monticello

Main Entrance

Dam

Boat Launch

Windmill Island

North Bog

Prairie Island

Heron Is.

Big Is.

Luther Lake

East Bay

Stonehouse Island

N

Wylde Lake

SCALE

0   1000   2000 metres

PINEHURST LAKE TRAIL

LOCATION: Pinehurst Lake Conservation Area, Cambridge
DISTANCE: 9 km/5.6 mi. loop (4 km/2.5 mi. loop option)
RATING: Beginner to intermediate
HIGHLIGHT: Kettle lake

TRAIL SURFACE: Hard-packed earth, grass.

DIRECTIONS: From Hwy. 401, take the Hwy. 24 South exit into Cambridge. Continue on Hwy. 24A/Regional Rd. 75 south towards Paris. After you pass Waterloo Regional Rd. 49, a sign is visible on your left.

MORE INFORMATION: (519) 442-4721. Admission fee applies.

Pinehurst Lake Conservation Area is in a region of "kettle" lakes, large holes that filled with the melt water of huge boulders of glacial ice.

The trails run around the lake, over hills and valleys and through pine and hardwood forest, looping into one another to create a long circuit.

The four-kilometre (2.5-mile) loop runs through a hardwood forest, circles the slightly rolling area around Pinehurst Lake and passes an 1800s mounted bell from Canning.

Continuing from this point, the pathway enters a rolling hardwood bush and continues to a white pine forest in the summer camping area. This five-kilometre (3.1- mile) trail passes through open spaces, ravines and valleys before veering to the right, and continuing through hardwood bush, wildflower meadows and white pine stands.

In open areas, look for a red-tailed hawk soaring overhead. In the forest, home to the great horned owl, you might hear the calls of chickadees, juncos and cardinals. Look closely to the side of the trail to find the tracks of a deer, fox or coyote.

In the winter, these trails are track set for cross-country skiers, marked as novice, intermediate and advanced.

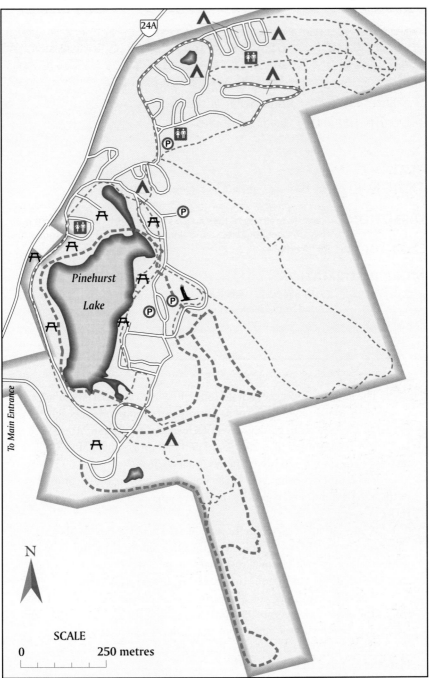

24A

Pinehurst Lake

To Main Entrance

N

SCALE

0   250 metres

R O C K W O O D   T R A I L

LOCATION: Rockwood Conservation Area, Rockwood
DISTANCE: 3.5 km/2.2 mi. linear
(Other Area Trails: partial loops)
RATING: Beginner to intermediate
HIGHLIGHT: Glacial potholes

TRAIL SURFACE: Hard-packed earth with rocks, tree roots and grass.

DIRECTIONS: From Hwy. 401, take the Guelph Line Exit north and turn right onto Hwy. 7. Continue until seeing signs for Rockwood Conservation Area on your right.

MORE INFORMATION:

(519) 856-9543. Admission fee applies.
Closed from Thanksgiving to May 1.

The Eramosa River meets limestone cliffs, caves and glacial potholes as it ambles its way through Rockwood. Twenty-three thousand years ago, the retreat of the Wisconsin glacier carved Rockwood Conservation Area's landscape, leaving more than 200 glacial potholes measuring up to six metres (20 feet) wide and twelve metres (40 feet) deep.

The trail starts behind the beach house with a steep, rocky climb, then heads into the forest and passes by the water's edge, a small cave and a large rock outcrop.

A large group of glacial potholes is located near the boardwalk area. Others can be seen from the lookout on the other side of the water. The glacial meltwaters swirled small rocks, large granite stones and sand with such force that they cut into the rock, creating these cylindrical holes.

From the boardwalk, you'll pass ruins of an old woollen and grist mill, run by the Harris family from 1867 to 1925. Within the interior of the ruin is a bridge crossing over a small brook that leads to a picnic area.

The rest of the trail leads through a forested area with one lookout that offers a grand view of the park.

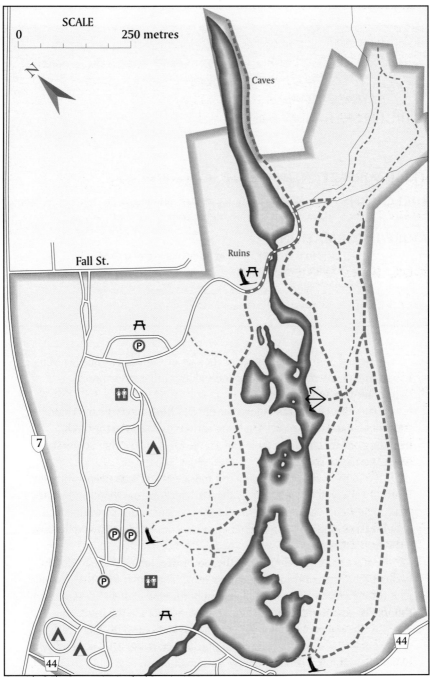

SCALE

0   250 metres

N

Caves

Fall St.

Ruins

7

44

44

SHADE'S MILLS TRAIL

LOCATION:	Shade's Mills Conservation Area, Cambridge
DISTANCE:	14 km/8.7 mi. loop (Other Area Trails: smaller interconnected loops)
RATING:	Beginner
HIGHLIGHT:	Sandy beach

TRAIL SURFACE: Wood mulch, hard-packed earth and grass.

DIRECTIONS: From Hwy. 401 East, take the Franklin Blvd. exit. Turn left on Avenue Road. Shade's Mills is on the right

MORE INFORMATION:

(519) 621-3697. Closed from Thanksgiving to May 1. Admission fee applies.

Located on the eastern edge of the City of Cambridge, Shade's Mills has a series of interconnected loop trails along with a sandy beach, swimming area and picnic spots.

The start of the trail follows the Shade's Mills reservoir and then continues along Mill Creek. There are various openings to the creek, including one with a picnic table and a large log that stretches across the creek - perfect to sit on!

From the creek, you'll pass a tree mosaic as you walk deeper into the forest. A variety of pines as well as shagbark hickory, basswood and white ash can be seen. The best time to spot the resident family of white-tailed deer is early in the morning when they move from bedding areas to feeding spots near the water.

After crossing Mill Creek on the footbridge, follow the map closely because there are many loops to choose from. They enter forested areas and pass through meadows where tall grasses border the path and daisies, thimbleweed, buttercup and bladder campion bloom in the fields.

At the northeast end of the loop, a trail leads down to Mill Creek, a great spot for brown trout fishing. In the 36-hectare (89-acre) reservoir, swim northern pike, perch and large and smallmouth bass.

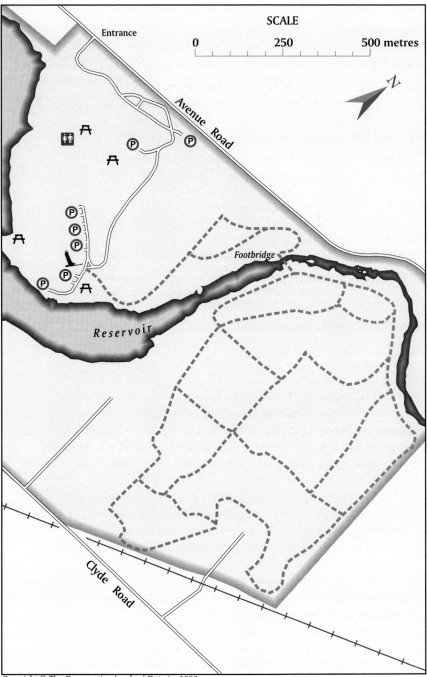

SCALE

0   250   500 metres

Entrance

Avenue Road

Footbridge

Reservoir

Clyde Road

N

CRAWFORD LAKE TRAILS

LOCATION: Crawford Lake Conservation Area, Milton

DISTANCE: 1.4 km/0.9 mi. Crawford Lake (Other Area Trails: 2.7 km/1.7 mi. Woodland, 2 km/1.2 mi. Pine Ridge, 2.6 km/1.6 mi. Escarpment Trail loop, 5 km/3.1 mi. Nassagaweya Trail to Rattlesnake Pt.)

RATING: Beginner to intermediate

HIGHLIGHT: Rare meromictic lake, escarpment lookouts, Iroquoian Village

LINK: Bruce Trail

TRAIL SURFACE: Hard-packed earth, gravel, rock and boardwalk.

DIRECTIONS: From Hwy. 401, take the Guelph Line south exit (Exit 312) to Steeles Ave., turn east to the park entrance. From the Q.E.W., take Guelph Line north (Exit 102) and turn east on Steeles Ave. to park entrance.

MORE INFORMATION: (905) 854-0234. Admission fee applies.

Located on top of the Niagara Escarpment, the rare meromictic Crawford Lake holds clues to the natural and cultural history of the Halton area. There is limited circulation and little oxygen below 15 metres (49 feet) in the lake and its stratified water doesn't circulate completely during the year. Microscopic pollen grains in bottom sediment led archeologists to find a nearby native village in 1971.

The Crawford Lake Trail circles the lake with three observation platforms. Interpretive signs on the natural history of the lake describe the unique organisms that live beneath its green, tranquil surface. Water activities are prohibited to preserve the delicate balance in the lake's ecosystem.

You may spot rare yellow lady's slippers, maidenhair spleenwort ferns and roundleaf sundew in this conservation area. There's also a small bog community complete with sphagnum moss.

The Woodland, Pine Ridge and Escarpment Trails venture beyond the lake into extensive woodlands, open meadows, pine plantations and along the brow of the escarpment. The Nassagaweya Trail crosses the Nassagaweya Canyon and leads to Rattlesnake Point Conservation Area.

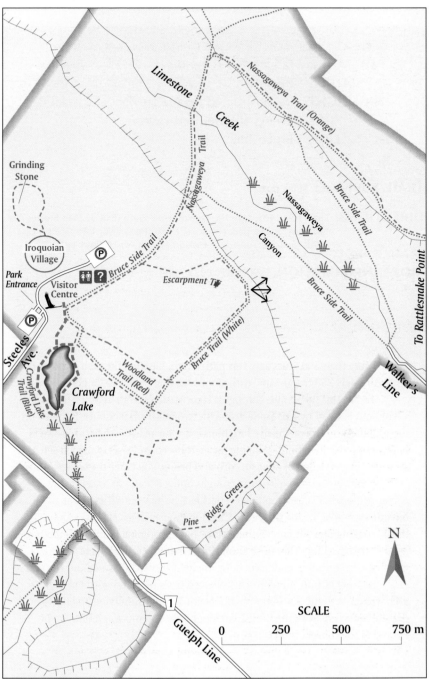

Grinding Stone

Iroquoian Village

Park Entrance

Steeles Ave.

Visitor Centre

Limestone

Creek

Nassagaweya Trail (Orange)

Nassagaweya Trail

Bruce Side Trail

Nassagaweya

Canyon

Bruce Side Trail

To Rattlesnake Point

Walker's Line

Bruce Side Trail

Escarpment Tr.

Bruce Trail (White)

Woodland Trail (Red)

Crawford Lake Trail (Blue)

Crawford Lake

Pine Ridge Green

1

Guelph Line

N

SCALE

0   250   500   750 m

Copyright © The Conservation Lands of Ontario, 1998

35

IROQUOIAN VILLAGE TRAIL

LOCATION: Crawford Lake Conservation Area, Milton
DISTANCE: 0.5 km/0.3 mi. loop
RATING: Beginner
HIGHLIGHT: Reconstructed Iroquoian village, special events and demonstrations
LINK: Bruce Trail

TRAIL SURFACE: Stone dust.

DIRECTIONS: From Hwy. 401, take the Guelph Line south (Exit 312) to Steeles Ave., turn east to the park entrance. From the Q.E.W., take Guelph Line north (Exit 102) and turn east on Steeles Ave. to park entrance.

MORE INFORMATION: (905) 854-0234 Admission fee applies.

More than 500 years ago, this path would have led through a village of approximately 250 Iroquoians, with smoke trailing from five longhouses.

Today, this trail winds through a reconstructed 15th-century Iroquoian village surrounded by a palisade wall with two platform lookouts. Situated on the original site, two of the five longhouses are furnished, while three others have been partially rebuilt. Walking past a tobacco and sweetgrass garden and another village garden of squash, corn and beans, you enter the village centre.

Hunting racks, maple syrup troughs and a woodcraft area portray village activities. Visitors can make a necklace or play native games at an outside craft area. Inside the Turtle Clan longhouse, items such as animal hides, cooking utensils and clothing show how aboriginal families would have lived in this dwelling. Demonstrations for activities such as maple sugar making, corn grinding and firemaking are held regularly throughout the year.

A study of bottom sediment collected from rare Crawford Lake led archaeologists to the discovery of this site in 1971. A simulated archaeological dig site is on display in the Wolf Clan longhouse and more exhibits can be viewed in the conservation centre.

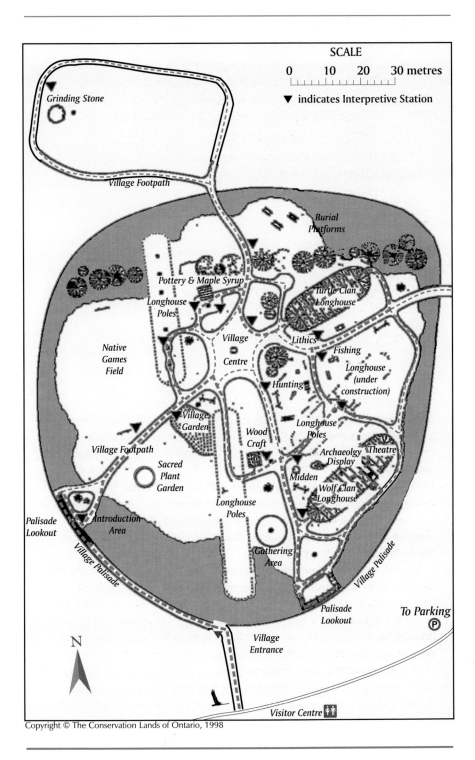

SCALE

0   10   20   30 metres

▼ indicates Interpretive Station

Grinding Stone

Village Footpath

Burial Platforms

Pottery & Maple Syrup

Turtle Clan Longhouse

Longhouse Poles

Native Games Field

Village Centre

Lithics

Fishing

Hunting

Longhouse (under construction)

Village Garden

Longhouse Poles

Village Footpath

Wood Craft

Archaeolgy Display

Theatre

Sacred Plant Garden

Midden

Introduction Area

Wolf Clan Longhouse

Palisade Lookout

Longhouse Poles

Gathering Area

Village Palisade

Village Palisade

Palisade Lookout

To Parking
Ⓟ

N

Village Entrance

Visitor Centre

HILTON FALLS TRAILS

LOCATION: Hilton Falls Conservation Area, Milton
DISTANCE: 4 km/2.5 mi. Hilton Falls (Other Area Trails: 2 km/1.2 mi. Red Oak, 9.5 km/6 mi. Beaver Dam Trail loops)
RATING: Beginner to intermediate
HIGHLIGHT: Waterfall, mill ruins
LINK: Bruce Trail

TRAIL SURFACE: Gravel, hard-packed earth and rocks.

DIRECTIONS: From Hwy. 401 take Guelph Line north (Exit 312) to Campbellville Rd., turn east to the park entrance. From the Q.E.W., take Guelph Line north (Exit 102) to Campbellville Road, turn east to park entrance.

MORE INFORMATION: (905) 854-0262. Admission fee applies.

Formed more than 12,000 years ago as meltwaters from retreating glaciers flowed over the escarpment, Hilton Falls cascades over a 10-metre (32.8 foot) drop, rushing past the scattered ruins of three 19th-century sawmills.

Remnants of the raceway channel, mill walls and a diversion dam can still be seen above the falls. From a viewing platform, you'll see the raceway arch, part of a wall that held a 12 metre (40 foot) mill wheel. Only small portions of the mill race wall remain, along with part of a cut stone dam above the falls.

There are myths and legends connected with the old mill. Hilton Falls was thought to be a stop on the underground railroad and the site of a hidden treasure of gold.

Beyond the falls, along part of the Bruce Trail, is a pothole worn in the bedrock. More than 12,000 years old, it was formed by loose stones being spun around in the force of the meltwaters.

The Hilton Falls trail connects with the Red Oak and the Beaver Dam trails, creating 16 kilometres (9.9 miles) of trails that weave past wooded swamps, beaver ponds and wetland pools where you may see the rare fruited bur-reed, yellow lady's slipper or the walking fern

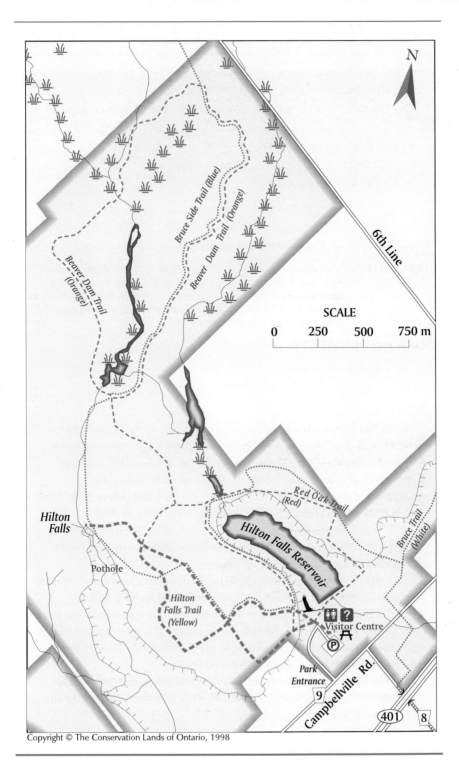

N

SCALE

0   250   500   750 m

6th Line

Bruce Side Trail (Blue)

Beaver Dam Trail (Orange)

Beaver Dam Trail (Orange)

Red Oak Trail (Red)

Hilton Falls Reservoir

Bruce Trail (White)

Hilton Falls

Pothole

Hilton Falls Trail (Yellow)

Visitor Centre

P

Park Entrance

9

Campbellville Rd.

401

8

KELSO/GLEN EDEN TRAILS

LOCATION:	Kelso/Glen Eden Conservation Area, Milton
DISTANCE:	6 km/3.7 mi. loop (Other Area Trails intersect main hiking trail)
RATING:	Intermediate
HIGHLIGHT:	Escarpment lookouts, lime kilns
LINK:	Bruce Trail

TRAIL SURFACE: Hard-packed earth, pavement.

DIRECTIONS: From the 401, take Hwy. 25 north (Exit 320) to Campbellville Rd. Turn west to Tremaine Rd. and west on Kelso Rd. to the park entrance. From the Q.E.W., take Hwy. 25 north (Exit 111) and turn west on Derry Rd. Turn north on Tremaine Rd., west on Kelso Rd. and continue to the park entrance.

MORE INFORMATION: (905) 878-5011. Fee applies.

Before winter arrives and downhill skiers rush to the slopes, take to the trails that lead beyond the chairlifts and continue deep into the forest. Starting to the east of the ski lodge, you pass the former Robertson Lime Kilns and Quarry on the steep ascent. The climb to the top of the escarpment is worth the view. From here, the abandoned quarry floor is still visible among trees and plants that are slowly reclaiming the site.

The trails beyond the escarpment edge intersect at various points, leading into open fields and through dense forest. Stay on the lookout for farmstead and lime kiln ruins along the way.

Parts of the trail system at the Kelso/Glen Eden Conservation Area are geared towards mountain bikers, so that certain trail sections such as Downhill Digger, have a cushion around a tree and straw bales banking steep and tight corners. Many of the trail sections are challenging and technically difficult – Grunt Climb, Rocky Downhill and Hawthorn Run among them. Another series of trails is designated for hikers only.

The Halton Region Museum's historical and Victorian exhibits are worth the visit. Located north of Day Lodge, the museum occupies the site of the former Alexander family farm.

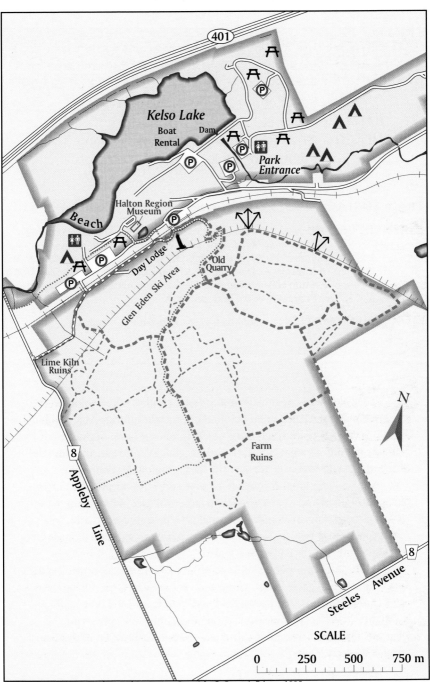

Source: Ontario Ministry of Natural Resources, Copyright © Queen's Printer, 1998

MOUNTSBERG TRAILS

LOCATION: Mountsberg Conservation Area, Campbellville

DISTANCE: Lakeshore Lookout Trail 5.6 km/3.5 mi. (6.5 km/4 mi. Pioneer Creek Trail, 1.5 km/0.9 mi. Sugar Bush Loop, 1 km/0.6 Nature Trivia Trail)

RATING: Beginner

HIGHLIGHT: Observation towers, waterfowl viewing, special events and maple syrup demonstration

TRAIL SURFACE: Hard-packed earth, grass.

DIRECTIONS: From Hwy. 401, take Guelph Line south (Exit 312) and turn west onto Reid Side Road. Turn south on Second Side Road, west on Campbellville Rd. and north on Milborough Line and continue to the park entrance. From the Q.E.W., take Guelph Line north (Exit 102) and turn west on Campbellville Rd. Turn north on Milborough Line and continue to the park entrance.

MORE INFORMATION: (905) 854-2276. Admission fee applies.

The Lakeshore Lookout Trail starts near swallowville, a colony of 150 tree swallows that dart through the shoreline meadow during May and June. From this vantage point you can see waterfowl on the Lake. Herons wade for fish near the water's edge, northern harriers glide silently over the contours of the marsh and osprey hover over the lake, scanning for fish below.

The trail continues through a red pine and white spruce plantation, an old apple orchard and then a wooded marsh. Discover old foundations and rock piles bordering an abandoned farmer's field. In the woodland, you might spot orange-crowned and hooded warblers, among the 218 bird species recorded at the conservation area.

At the trail's midpoint stands an observation tower, a prime viewing area for ducks and geese in the spring and various shorebirds during the fall.

Amid wetlands, overgrown fields and ponds, an 1860 lime kiln highlights the Pioneer Creek Trail. Along this pathway, lies the trunk of what was the largest trembling aspen tree in Ontario, before a 1978 storm toppled the leafy giant.

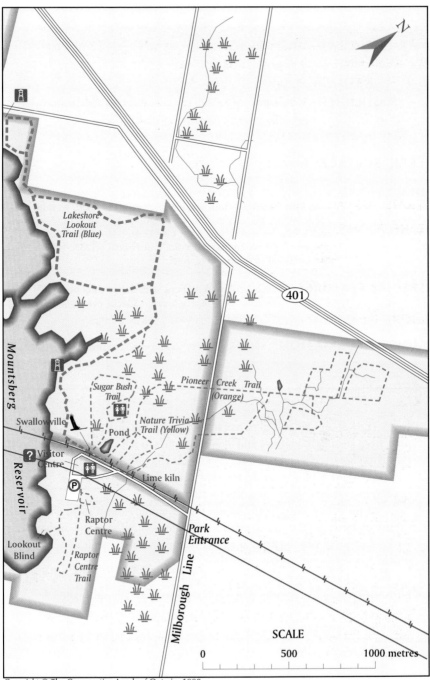

401

Lakeshore
Lookout
Trail (Blue)

Mountsberg

Pioneer Creek Trail
(Orange)

Sugar Bush
Trail

Nature Trivia
Trail (Yellow)

Swallowville

Pond

Reservoir

Visitor
Centre

Lime kiln

Raptor
Centre

Park
Entrance

Lookout
Blind

Raptor
Centre
Trail

Milborough Line

SCALE

0   500   1000 metres

RAPTOR CENTRE TRAIL

LOCATION:	Mountsberg Conservation Area, Campbellville
DISTANCE:	1.6 km/1 mi.
RATING:	Beginner
HIGHLIGHT:	Live birds of prey; special events, demonstrations and live birds of prey presentations

TRAIL SURFACE: Stone dust.

DIRECTIONS: From Hwy. 401, take Guelph Line south (Exit 312) and turn west onto Reid Side Road. Turn south on Second Side Road, west on Campbellville Rd. and north on Milborough Line and continue to the park entrance. From the Q.E.W., take Guelph Line north (Exit 102) and turn west on Campbellville Rd. Turn north on Milborough Line and continue to the park entrance.

SPECIAL FEATURES: Educational presentations with live birds of prey are available in the raptor flyway. Special events and demonstrations.

MORE INFORMATION: (905) 854-2276. Admission fee applies.

The Raptor Centre trail passes several enclosures holding birds of prey, from kestrels to vultures and long-eared owls to red-tailed hawks. Percheron horses, elk and bison are also visible along the trail. There is a waterfowl viewing blind near the reservoir for observing wood ducks, hooded mergansers, osprey and other waterfowl.

At the end of the trail, the Raptor Centre has an exhibit gallery, video theatre on birds of prey and an avian hospital for injured, sick and orphaned birds. A one-way viewing window allows visitors to watch medical procedures without disturbing the birds.

After treatment, most birds are rehabilitated and returned to the wild. Birds with permanent injuries that can't be released are placed in special enclosures on the raptor centre trail and used in programs to teach people about the importance of raptors.

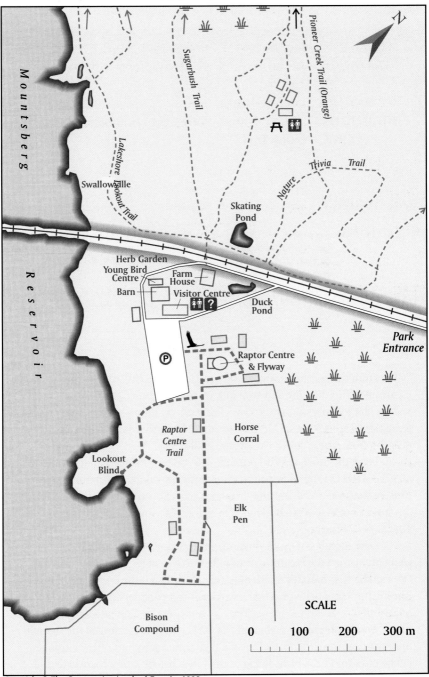

Mountsberg

Reservoir

Pioneer Creek Trail (Orange)

Sugarbush Trail

Lakeshore Lookout Trail

Swallowville

Trivia Trail

Nature

Skating Pond

Herb Garden

Young Bird Centre

Farm House

Barn

Visitor Centre

Duck Pond

Park Entrance

Raptor Centre & Flyway

Raptor Centre Trail

Horse Corral

Lookout Blind

Elk Pen

Bison Compound

SCALE

0   100   200   300 m

Copyright © The Conservation Lands of Ontario, 1998

MOUNT NEMO TRAILS

LOCATION: Mount Nemo Conservation Area, Burlington
DISTANCE: 2.3 km/1.4 mi. north loop and 2.6 km/ 1.6 mi. south loop
RATING: Intermediate
HIGHLIGHT: Large number of escarpment lookouts
LINK: Bruce Trail

TRAIL SURFACE: Hard-packed earth, rocks and grass.

DIRECTIONS: From Hwy. 401 take Guelph Line south (Exit 312), turn east on Colling Rd. and continue to the park entrance. From the Q.E.W. take Guelph Line north (Exit 102), turn east at Colling Rd. to park entrance.

MORE INFORMATION: (905) 336-1158. Admission fee applies.

From the gnarled, eastern white cedars on the cliff edge to the escarpment forest below, this trail follows the escarpment rim, with spectacular lookouts along the way. The pathway passes crevice caves, rock fissures and talus slopes. Moss-covered boulders with ferns and small trees growing from cracks soften the rugged landscape.

From the Brock Harris Lookout, 295 metres (968 feet) above sea level, 50 kilometres (31 miles) of countryside come into view. The communities of Milton, Brampton and Toronto, Nassagaweya Canyon and Rattlesnake Point are spread out across the horizon. On a clear day, you can even spot Toronto's CN Tower.

Over millions of years, erosion, glaciers, ancient rivers and the elements shaped the escarpment into distinctive craggy cliffs and rugged slopes. The return on the south loop turns away from the limestone bluffs, leading through open meadows, a narrow forest corridor and a former quarry site.

Another highlight is the sight of turkey vultures gliding in the thermal updrafts near the cliffs. Standing at a higher vantage point offers a unique perspective to see the birds flying in the valley below, rather than watching them soar above.

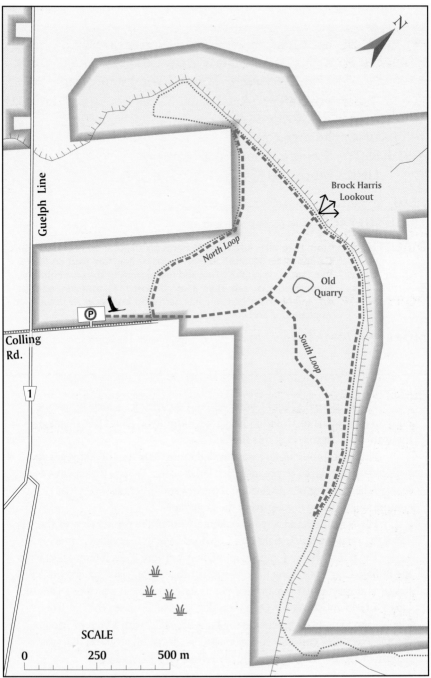

Guelph Line

Colling
Rd.

1

Brock Harris
Lookout

Old
Quarry

North Loop

South Loop

SCALE

0   250   500 m

Source: Ontario Ministry of Natural Resources, © Queen's Printer, 1998

RATTLESNAKE POINT TRAILS

LOCATION: Rattlesnake Point Conservation Area, Milton
DISTANCE: 3 km/1.9 mi. Buffalo Crag (Other Area Trails: 1 km/0.6 Rabbit's Run, 1.5 km/0.9 mi. Vista Adventure, 5 km/3.1 mi. Nassagaweya Canyon Trail to Crawford Lake)
RATING: Intermediate
HIGHLIGHT: Scenic lookouts, rock climbing
LINK: Bruce Trail

TRAIL SURFACE: Hard-packed earth and rock.

DIRECTIONS: From Hwy. 401, take Hwy. 25 north (Exit 320), turn west on Campbellville Rd. and south on Tremaine Rd. Turn west on Steeles Ave., south on Appleby Line and follow signs to the park entrance. From the Q.E.W., take Hwy. 25 north (Exit 111), turn west on Derry Rd. and north on Tremaine Rd. Turn west on Steeles Ave., south on Appleby Line and continue to park entrance.

MORE INFORMATION: (905) 878-1147. Admission Fee applies.

The Rattlesnake Point Conservation Area includes a huge limestone outcrop that is part of Ontario's Niagara Escarpment. Don't fear the name, there are no rattlesnakes at this site!

This limestone cliff-face was formed more than 400 million years ago, sculpted by pre-glacial rivers and glacial meltwater. Within the crevices and fissures there are numerous ferns and mosses and other unusual plant communities that have adapted to the landscape.

The Nassagaweya Canyon Lookout provides a sweeping view of the valley between the Rattlesnake and Crawford Lake Conservation Areas.

The Nassagaweya Canyon and Vista Adventure trails interconnect with the Buffalo Crag Trail along the escarpment edge. The Vista Adventure Trail has several spectacular lookout points. Trafalgar Lookout provides a view of Lake Ontario and Toronto. On a clear day, you can even see the CN Tower. The Nelson lookout is directed to the Lowville valley with a view of Mount Nemo. The valley entrance is surrounded by glacial till or gravel that was deposited 12,000 years ago during the retreat of the last glacier.

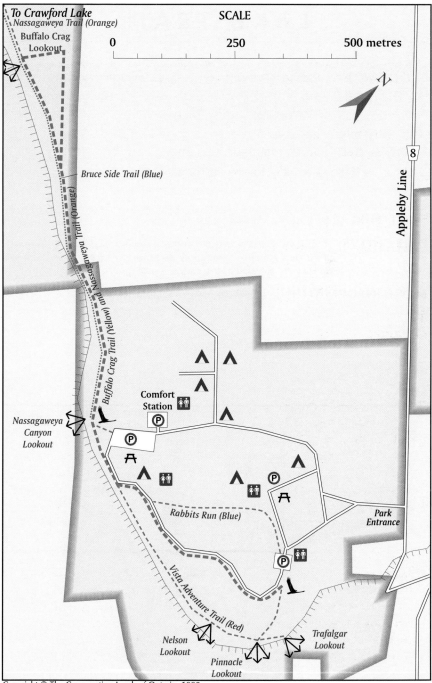

To Crawford Lake
Nassagaweya Trail (Orange)
Buffalo Crag Lookout

SCALE

0   250   500 metres

8

Appleby Line

Bruce Side Trail (Blue)

Nassagaweya Trail (Orange)

Buffalo Crag Trail (Yellow) and Nassagaweya Trail (Orange)

Comfort Station

P

P

Nassagaweya Canyon Lookout

P

P

Rabbits Run (Blue)

P

Park Entrance

Vista Adventure Trail (Red)

Nelson Lookout

Pinnacle Lookout

Trafalgar Lookout

Copyright © The Conservation Lands of Ontario, 1998

49

CHRISTIE 'ROUND-THE-LAKE TRAIL

LOCATION:	Christie Conservation Area, Flamborough
DISTANCE:	5.6 km/3.5 mi. loop (Other Area Trails: 3 km/ 1.9 mi. Wilderness Trail)
RATING:	Beginner
HIGHLIGHT:	Prairie plantation patch
LINK:	Crook's Hollow Historical Trail

TRAIL SURFACE: Hard-packed earth, grass.

DIRECTIONS: From Hwy. 401 take Hwy.6 South and turn right on Hwy. 5. Turn left at the park entrance. From Hwy. 403 take Hwy. 6 North and turn left on Hwy. 5. Turn left at the park entrance.

MORE INFORMATION: (905) 628-3060. Admission fee applies.

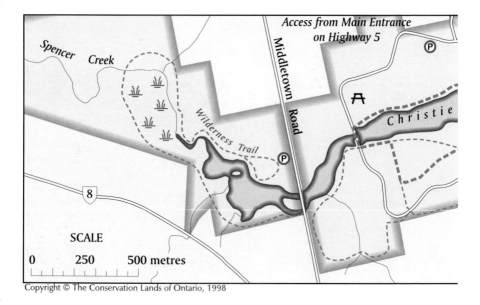

On top of the Niagara Escarpment, 10 kilometres (6.2 miles) of trails wind through peaceful meadows, rolling hills and upland forests surrounding a wetland and a calm, 61-hectare (151-acre) lake. Supporting remnant natural communities of cattail marsh, cedar swamp and broadleaf swamp, this area also has a prairie plantation patch. Planted on the site of a former oak savannah, black-eyed susans, blazing stars and purple coneflowers wave among big blue stem and Indian grasses.

You'll pass this prairie patch on the north side of the lake when you start the trail. Walking across the nine-metre (30-foot) high Christie Dam offers the best view of the lake. From here, enter a woodland area where you catch glimpses of the lake through some of the trees. Rolling hills and steep slopes wind through a pine plantation where green ferns dot the soft, needle-covered ground. This trail also joins the Wedeln Run, Lowland and Wilderness Trails. These interlinking spots are easy to identify with names and symbols written on the sides of wooden posts.

Although this trail is called 'Round-the-Lake, the pathway is mostly in the forest until crossing the bridge near Middletown Road. Along the lakeshore, gulls pace near picnic tables and herons wade near the water's edge. On this north side, nine stocked trout ponds are nestled among sedges.

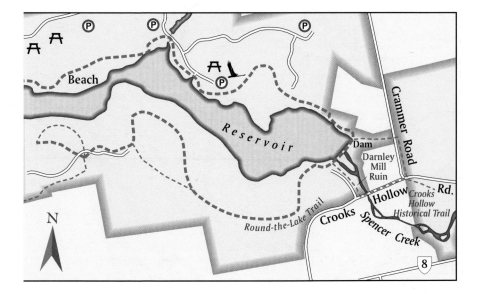

CROOKS' HOLLOW
HISTORICAL TRAIL

LOCATION:	Crooks' Hollow Conservation Area, Greensville
DISTANCE:	1.5 km/0.9 mi. loop (Other Area Trails: 2 km from Crooks' Hollow Rd. to Spencer Gorge)
RATING:	Beginner
HIGHLIGHT:	Historical
LINK:	Bruce Trail, Christie Conservation Area, Spencer Gorge, Tew's and Webster's Falls, historic Greensville

TRAIL SURFACE:
>Hard-packed earth.

DIRECTIONS: From Hwy. 401 take Hwy.6 South and turn right on Hwy. 5. Turn left on Brock Rd. and right on Old Brock Rd. into Greensville. Old Brock Rd. curves to the right but drive straight through the intersection to reach Crooks' Hollow Conservation Area, the 2nd parking lot on your left-hand side. From Hwy. 403 take Hwy. 6 North and turn left on Hwy. 5.

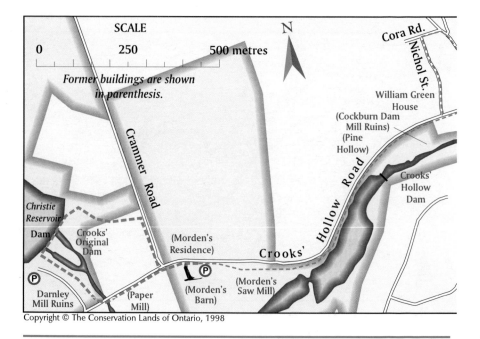

SCALE

0   250   500 metres

N

Former buildings are shown in parenthesis.

Cora Rd.

Nichol St.

William Green House
(Cockburn Dam Mill Ruins)
(Pine Hollow)

Crammer Road

Crooks' Hollow Dam

Christie Reservoir

Dam

Crooks' Original Dam

(Morden's Residence)

Hollow Road

Crooks'

(P)

Darnley Mill Ruins

(Paper Mill)

(Morden's Barn)

(Morden's Saw Mill)

(P)

Copyright © The Conservation Lands of Ontario, 1998

This trail follows Spencer Creek as the waterway slowly meanders along a shallowly incised bedrock valley. Difficult to imagine that quiet Crooks' Hollow was once one of the largest industrial communities in Upper Canada.

It all started in 1801, when Jonathan Morden built the first sawmill on the upper section of Spencer Creek. Between 1820 and 1850, James Crooks harnessed the available water power to establish several industries along Crooks' Hollow Road and Spencer Creek.

This historical trail, weaving from forest to roadway, leads to many of these historic mill sites. From the present Christie Dam, remnants of Crooks' original stone dam and mill race can still be seen.

At one time, there were 18 mills along the creek. Darnley Mill, which supplied flour to the British Army during the War of 1812, is the only one still standing. Across the road, an 1840s log cabin, one of several built by Crooks for his workers, still stands. A heritage plaque marks Upper Canada's first papermill, built by Crooks in 1826.

You have the option of following a linear trail along Crooks' Hollow Road into the historic village of Greensville. This trail leads to Spencer Gorge and Webster's Falls, linking with the Bruce Trail.

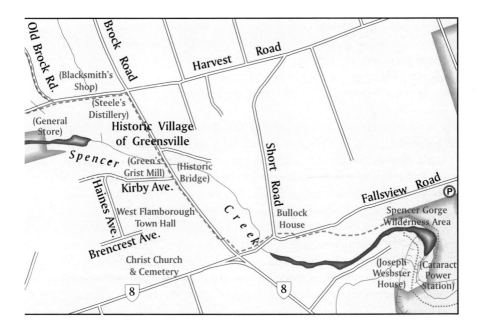

DUNDAS VALLEY TRAILS

LOCATION: Dundas Valley Conservation Area, Dundas
DISTANCE: 3 km/1.9 mi. main loop (Other Area Trails: Please refer to the Dundas Valley Trail Guide)
RATING: Beginner to intermediate
HIGHLIGHT: Niagara Escarpment, Carolinian forest, Hermitage Ruins, Griffin House, reproduction Victorian Train station
LINK: Bruce Trail

TRAIL SURFACE: Gravel and hard-packed earth.

DIRECTIONS: From 403, take Hwy. 52 to Copetown, turn right on Governors Rd. (Regional Rd. 299) to the main entrance of the Conservation area. From Hwy. 401, take Hwy. 6 South to Hwy. 403 West towards Hamilton. Take the Main Street West exit to Dundas. Turn left on Main St. and follow into Dundas. Turn left on Governors Rd. and follow signs to the Dundas Valley Conservation Area.

MORE INFORMATION: Visitor Center (905) 627-1233. For trail conditions check www.hamrca.on.ca or call 1-888-319-HRCA. Admission fee applies.

More than 40 kilometres (24.9 miles) of trails pass through the Dundas Valley among 1,012 hectares (2,500 acres) of Carolinian forest and hemlock groves, stream and marsh valleys, historical ruins and rugged Niagara Escarpment hills. For safe hiking among these connecting trails, purchase a Dundas Valley Trail Map at the Visitor Centre, a reproduction Victorian railway station.

Start from the Visitor Centre on the Main Loop Trail, where you'll pass a sulphur spring, once pumped into a local hotel for spa treatments. Next, walk through the ruins of the Hermitage, an 1855 summer estate for the Leith family. Stop at the Gatehouse Museum, part of the original estate that housed the gatekeeper and his family. The museum now exhibits artifacts excavated from the ruins and a model of the Hermitage mansion.

From the Orchard Trail, stroll into a stream valley with rare plants such as the walking fern, green violet and yellow mandarin before reaching an old apple orchard. After travelling through the Merrick Orchard, you'll pass the Apple Cider Shanty. Rest in a nearby clearing on two benches under a large oak tree border before beginning the return descent to the Visitor Centre.

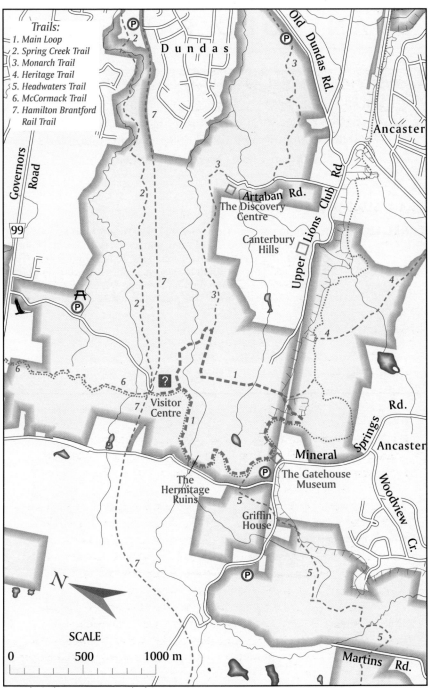

Trails:
1. Main Loop
2. Spring Creek Trail
3. Monarch Trail
4. Heritage Trail
5. Headwaters Trail
6. McCormack Trail
7. Hamilton Brantford
   Rail Trail

Dundas

Old Dundas Rd.

Ancaster

Governors Road

99

Artaban Rd.

The Discovery Centre

Canterbury Hills

Upper Lions Club Rd.

Visitor Centre

Mineral

Springs

Ancaster

Rd.

The Gatehouse Museum

The Hermitage Ruins

Griffin House

Woodview Cr.

N

SCALE

0   500   1000 m

Martins   Rd.

Copyright © The Conservation Lands of Ontario, 1998

HAMILTON TO
BRANTFORD RAIL TRAIL

DISTANCE: 32 km/19.9 mi. linear
RATING: Beginner
HIGHLIGHT: Passes through Dundas Valley Conservation Area
LINK: Hamilton Wentworth Bikeway and Brantford's Gordon Glaves Memorial Pathway.

TRAIL SURFACE: Stone dust.

DIRECTIONS: To Hamilton Access: From Hwy. 403, take Hwy. 8 Main St. West (past McMaster University). Travel 2 km, turn left on Ewen Rd. and right on Ofield Rd. The parking lot is on your right. To Brantford Access: From the 401, take Hwy. 24 South to Hwy. 403 East. Exit south on Gordon Ave. to Colborne St. Turn right on Colborne, left on Locks Road, and right on Greenwich Street. The parking lot will be on your left.

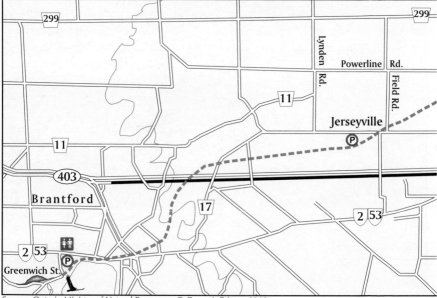

Source: Ontario Ministry of Natural Resources, © Queen's Printer, 1998

This converted railway line, the first off-road, inter-urban trail linking two major cities in Ontario, descends on a 3% grade through the Niagara Escarpment to the Grand River's scenic banks. On this trail you'll cross Binkley Hollow, a naturalized embankment that covers a wooden trestle bridge, and pass the remains of the 1986 Brantford landslide.

The trail begins near Hamilton's McMaster University and leads through part of the city before entering Dundas Valley Conservation Area. For exhibits of the area, stop at the visitor centre, a reproduction Victorian train station. From here, the next 27 kilometres (16.7 miles) continue westward towards Brantford.

A few kilometres from the visitor centre there's a lookout and interpretive display for Summit Bog, a rare spruce and tamarack bog. The lookout includes a remnant cistern cylinder where steam trains filled up with water after the steep climb.

From this point, the trail ambles by farm pastures and thick woodlots, crosses under Hwy. 403 and follows Fairchild Creek towards the Grand River valley. The final descent to the river was once a difficult climb for trains of the Toronto, Hamilton and Buffalo Railway.

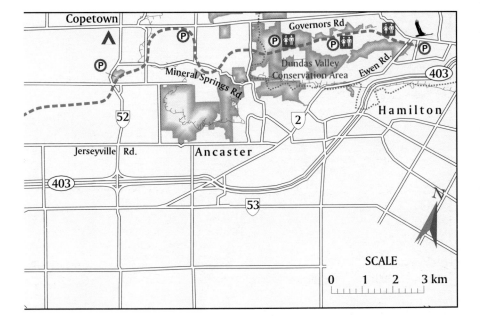

RED HILL VALLEY
RECREATIONAL TRAIL

LOCATION: Red Hill Valley, Hamilton
DISTANCE: 7 km./4.3 mi. linear
RATING: Beginner to intermediate
HIGHLIGHT: Carolinian forest
LINK: Hamilton Wentworth Regional Bikeway
Trail, Waterfront Trail, Bruce Trail

TRAIL SURFACE: Stone dust, tar and chip.

DIRECTIONS: From Hwy. 401 take Hwy. 6 South to the 403 Hamilton. Take the L.M. Alexander Expressway towards Hamilton. Exit at Dartnall Road, turn left on Stone Church Rd. and left on Pritchard Rd. Turn right on Mud St. and enter the parking lot on your left. For waterfalls, exit right from the parking lot and follow Mud St. as it changes to Mountain Brow Boulevard. Park at King's Forest parking lot and walk along the road to the cement stairs that lead to its base. For Buttermilk Falls, turn right at the parking lot 0.4 km from the Mountain Brow Blvd. and Limeridge Rd. E. intersection. You can see the falls from the end of the yellow guard rail.

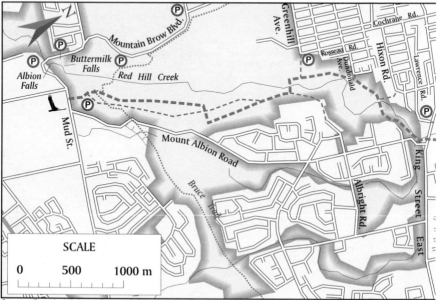

Source: Ontario Ministry of Natural Resources, © Queen's Printer, 1998

Nestled within the industrial city of Hamilton is a pocket of land alive with butterflies, breeding birds, reptiles and amphibians. As the last, large natural area within the city limits, the trail is lined with colourful thickets and steep banks of red clay that give the valley its name.

Native people once camped along Red Hill Creek to catch Atlantic salmon moving upstream. Today, it's home to 18 species of fish, filled with trout, northern pike and chinook salmon. Evidence of native fishing camps dates back 5,000 years. Archaeological digs have also unearthed areas used by United Empire Loyalists and European settlers.

Before you start the trail, stop to watch two ribbon waterfalls that cascade over the escarpment. Buttermilk Falls is visible from the roadside and Albion Falls is best experienced by taking a rough walk to the boulders at its base (directions below). A trail map and guide for Red Hill Valley is available from the Hamilton Region Conservation Authority.

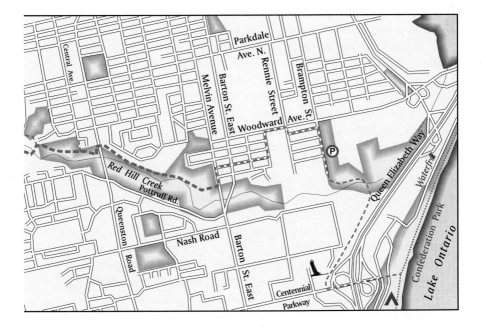

ROYAL BOTANICAL GARDENS NORTH SHORE TRAIL

LOCATION: Royal Botanical Gardens, Hamilton
DISTANCE: 3 km/1.9 mi. loop (Other Area Trails: 2.1 km/ 1.3 mi. Pinetum,2.9 km/1.8 mi. Captain Cootes)
RATING: Beginner
HIGHLIGHT: Cootes Paradise Nature Sanctuary, wetland exhibit
LINK: Bruce Trail

TRAIL SURFACE: Hard-packed earth.

DIRECTIONS: From Hwy. 401, take Hwy. 6 South. Turn left on Plains Rd. W. extension and follow signs for the Arboretum. Turn right on Old Guelph Rd.

SPECIAL FEATURES: Nature Interpretive Centre.

MORE INFORMATION: (905) 527-1158. Admission fee applies.

At the western end of Lake Ontario, 838 hectares (2,071 acres) of forest, field and marsh are nestled in Cootes Paradise Nature Sanctuary. More than 20 kilometres (12.4 miles) of nature trails lead through protected forests and along the wetlands and natural shorelines.

The trails lead by willow thickets, through cattail coves and pockets of Carolinian forest. Although located only 2 kilometres (1.2 miles) from downtown Hamilton, when you reach the viewing area at Bull's Point, the highway noise fades and the city seems miles away.

The site of an aboriginal seasonal fishing camp dating from 900 A.D., Cootes Paradise is now frequented by birders and nature lovers for sightings of black-crowned night herons, a cormorant colony and salamanders. It is also home to Project Paradise, one of the largest marsh restoration schemes on the Great Lakes.

From the Nature Interpretive Centre, start on the Captain Cootes Trail and walk along the shoreline. Connect with the Marsh Boardwalk to reach the viewing platform with a sweeping overview of the sanctuary. Trees are labeled along the Grey Doe Trail with varieties such as witch hazel, butternut and blue beech. From Grey Doe, either continue on the Homestead Trail to connect with the Pinetum and Bruce Trails or finish this shorter loop by walking up through the lilac dell, home to the world's largest collection of lilacs. The headquarters for the Bruce Trail Association are located on the grounds.

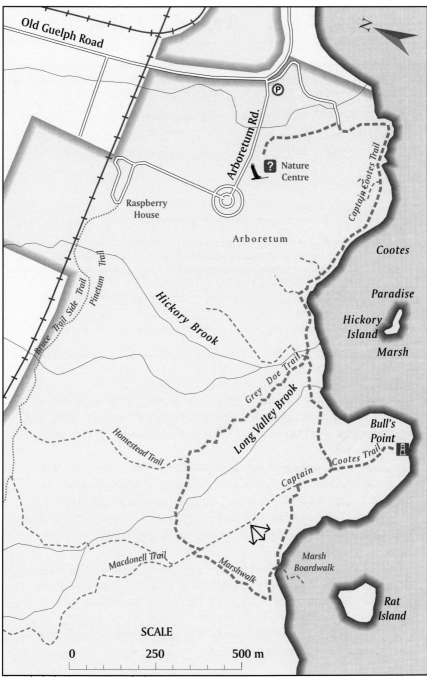

Old Guelph Road

Arboretum Rd.

? Nature
Centre

Raspberry
House

Arboretum

Hickory Brook

Bruce Trail Side Trail

Pinetum Trail

Grey Doe Trail

Long Valley Brook

Homestead Trail

Captain Cootes Trail

Captain

Cootes Trail

Macdonell Trail

Marshwalk

Cootes

Paradise

Hickory
Island

Marsh

Bull's
Point

Marsh
Boardwalk

Rat
Island

SCALE

0   250   500 m

SPENCER GORGE
WATERFALLS TRAIL

LOCATION: Spencer Gorge Wilderness Area, Greensville
DISTANCE: 6 km/3.7 mi. linear
RATING: Intermediate and advanced
HIGHLIGHT: Waterfalls
LINK: Bruce Trail, Crooks Hollow Historical Trail

TRAIL SURFACE: Hard-packed earth with tree roots and rocks.

DIRECTIONS: To reach Webster's Falls parking lot take Hwy. 8 from Dundas. Turn right on Brock Road and right at the flashing light onto Harvest Rd. Turn right onto Short Road and left onto Fallsview Rd and follow the signs for the parking lot. For Dundas Peak and Tew's Falls Lookout Parking, follow Harvest Rd. further down until you see the signs. A parking fee applies.

Spencer Gorge Wilderness Area is a Y-shaped bedrock gorge with two very scenic waterfalls. To reach Webster's Falls, follow the Bruce Trail from the parking lot and then continue on the Bruce Trail along the escarpment edge to Tew's Falls.

The bowl-shaped rock formation that this "ribbon falls" pours over and the gorge that Spencer Creek flows through were both formed by glacial meltwaters. Farther downstream, the gorge widens, suggesting that the falls were once as large as the Horseshoe Falls in Niagara. The gorge at Tew's Falls is 41 metres (134.5 feet) high and Horseshoe Falls is 52 metres (171 feet) high.

From Tew's Falls, the trail continues to the mouth of Spencer Gorge. At the tip, Dundas Peak offers a spectacular view of the Dundas Valley. In the distance lies Stoney Creek, Hamilton Harbour and landmarks such as McMaster University and Cootes Paradise.

The steep hike up to Webster's Falls along the Bruce trail makes the view from the top even more rewarding.

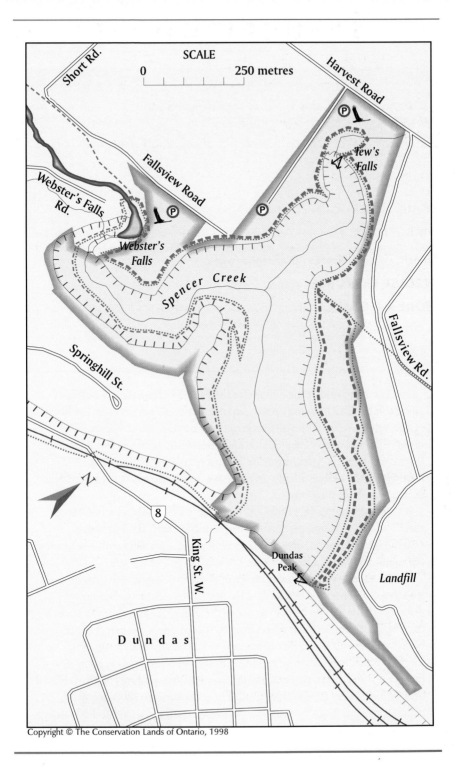

SCALE

0   250 metres

Short Rd.

Harvest Road

Fallsview Road

Webster's Falls Rd.

Webster's Falls

Tew's Falls

Spencer Creek

Fallsview Rd.

Springhill St.

N

8

King St. W.

Dundas Peak

Landfill

D u n d a s

VALENS BOARDWALK TRAIL

LOCATION: Valens Conservation Area, Freelton
DISTANCE: 4.2 km/2.6 mi. loop
RATING: Beginner
HIGHLIGHT: 5-storey observation platform

TRAIL SURFACE: Hard-packed earth, boardwalk, grass.

DIRECTIONS: From Hwy. 401, take Hwy. 6 South and turn right on Regional Road 97 and follow signs. From Hwy. 403, take Hwy. 6 North, turn left on Reg. Rd. 97 and follow signs..

SPECIAL FEATURES: Hunting season.

MORE INFORMATION: (905) 525-2183, fax (905) 659-1573. Admission fee applies.

The bench along the 300-metre (984-foot) boardwalk is a highlight along this trail. Set among cattails, marsh marigolds and irises in the heart of the Valens wetland, this sitting area offers an opportunity to quietly observe the waterfowl, amphibians and insects that thrive in this marsh and fish sanctuary. A frog leaps from a log and splashes into the water. A northern harrier glides silently over the marsh's contours. A bare tree trunk awaits a cavity nesting bird.

Ten kilometres (6.2 miles) of interconnecting trails take you from marsh and observation platform to maple forests and lakeshore edge. Leaving the boardwalk, divert to the maple walk, a winding pathway through tall maple trees with a lookout over the lake.

Eventually you reach the reservoir shoreline dotted with cattails and Joe Pyeweed. From the Wilderness Pavilion, turn right to walk along the reservoir to the fishing bridge. Cross to the other side and skirt the water's edge before re-entering the forest near the canoe dock. There's another boardwalk to walk along before heading to the observation tower.

Up the main road through the campground, you'll reach a five-storey high observation platform that towers over the surrounding countryside and nearby pine trees. Don't forget to stop in at the historic 1800s log cabin which houses such antiques as a wool winder, spinning wheel and oil lantern.

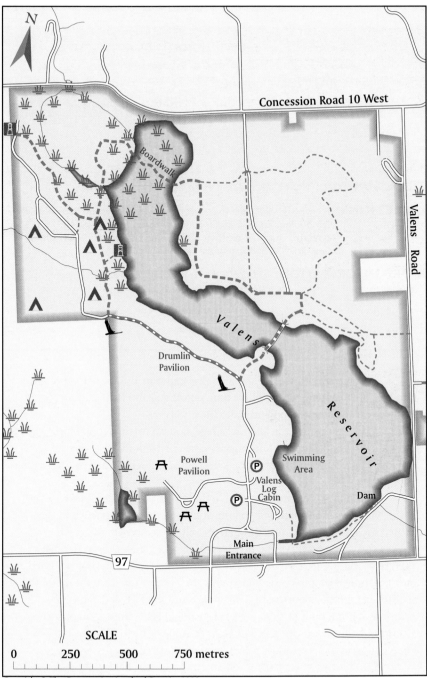

N

Concession Road 10 West

Valens Road

Boardwalk

V a l e n s

Drumlin
Pavilion

R e s e r v o i r

Powell
Pavilion

Swimming
Area

P

Valens
Log
Cabin

P

Dam

Main
Entrance

97

SCALE

0   250   500   750 metres

WESTFIELD HERITAGE TRAIL

LOCATION: Westfield Heritage Village, Rockton
DISTANCE: 1 km/0.6 mi. village trail
RATING: Beginner
HIGHLIGHT: 33 heritage buildings

TRAIL SURFACE: Gravel, hard-packed earth with rocks and grass.

DIRECTIONS: From Hwy. 401, take Hwy. 6 south and turn right on Regional Rd. 97, left on Reg. Rd. 552 and follow the signs. From Hwy. 403, take Hwy. 6 North. Turn left on Hwy. 5 and right on Hwy. 8. Turn right on Reg. Rd. 552 and follow the signs.

MORE INFORMATION: (519) 621-8851, fax (519) 621-6897. Admission fee applies.

The entrance to Westfield makes this trail walk unique. Pass through the tollgate to enter a village where time stands still and then skirt an old railway car to enter a woodland trail area.

Walking through the historic village, note an original mud block house, a log chapel used at Kanyengeh on the Six Nations Reserve until 1854, and an 1840s one-room log home. A brochure for a self-guided walking tour is available.

The village is open year round to trail users. The buildings are locked from Monday to Saturday, but you can still sense the atmosphere and learn about each historic structure through the self-guided brochure.

To visit on Sundays and holidays (March-December), is to step back 150 years. Buildings from the general store to the blacksmith shop are filled with costumed characters demonstrating their craft. You'll see the oldest log church in Ontario, a one-room schoolhouse and the T.H. & B. Jerseyville Railway Station, built in 1896. The village might also remind you of scenes from the Sullivan television productions of Anne of Green Gables and Road to Avonlea, as many episodes were filmed on the premises.

Don't forget to walk the woodland trail, starting behind the railroad station.

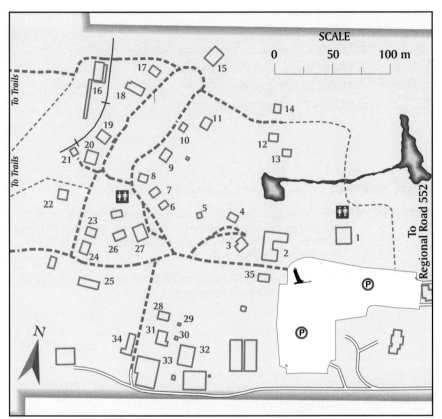

Heritage Buildings

1. Potts Building
2. The Ironwood Tea House
3. Blacksmith Shop
4. Log House
5. Bake Oven
6. Edmundson House
7. Marr Shop
8. Seth Fothergill's Print Shop
9. Misener House
10. Albrecht Seip Boot & Harness Shop
11. Bamberger House
12. Log Chapel
13. Log Home
14. Trading Post
15. Mountsberg Church
16. Jerseyville Railway Station
17. Drug Store
18. Gillen House
19. McRoberts Dry Goods Store
20. General Store
21. Ice House
22. Cathcart School No. 24
23. George Potts' Spinning Wheel Shop
24. Cabinetmaker's Shop
25. Sawmill
26. Inn Drive Shed
27. D'Aubigny Inn
28. Lockhart Log House
29. Smokehouse
30. Log Outhouse
31. Farm Barn
32. Carriage Barn
33. Agricultural Barn
34. Farm Drive Shed
35. Gift Shop

WESTFIELD WOODS TRAIL

LOCATION: Westfield Heritage Village, Rockton
DISTANCE: 5 km/3.1 mi. loop
RATING: Beginner
HIGHLIGHT: Barn ruins, alvar

TRAIL SURFACE: Gravel, hard-packed earth with rocks and grass.

DIRECTIONS: From Hwy. 401, take Hwy. 6 south and turn right on Regional Rd. 97, left on Reg. Rd. 552 and follow the signs. From Hwy. 403, take Hwy. 6 North. Turn left on Hwy. 5 and right on Hwy. 8. Turn right on Reg. Rd. 552 and follow the signs.

MORE INFORMATION: (519) 621-8851, fax (519) 621-6897. Admission fee applies.

Even a walk through the woods behind Westfield Heritage Village offers discoveries of a bygone era. The trail starts behind the railroad station, passes a sugar shack and leads to a T-intersection. Turn right and continue walking until a path opens on your left.

The trail meanders through 131 hectares (324 acres) filled with coniferous and deciduous forests, marshland, thick lilac patches and alvar full of fragrant sumacs. Scattered throughout are farm ruins dating back to the mid-1800s. You'll find the largest ruin behind the sprawling branches of an old oak tree towards the end of the trail. Surrounding a large mound are fenceposts, barn foundation marks and trees growing from outbuilding ruins.

From this ruin, follow the gravel road to the left. By turning right, you enter a swampy area and the trail eventually ends. As you complete this loop, the gravel road follows a stone wall, rocks that once lined a farmer's field. Keep your eyes peeled for a giant swallowtail, northern ribbon snake or Cooper's hawk.

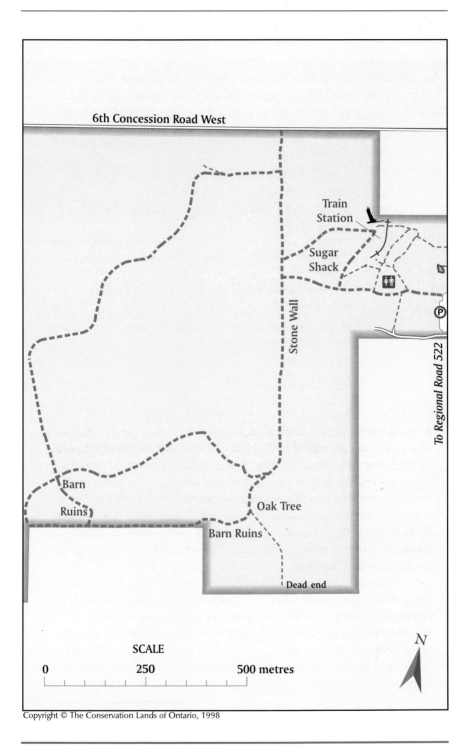

6th Concession Road West

Train Station

Sugar Shack

Stone Wall

To Regional Road 522

Barn Ruins

Oak Tree

Barn Ruins

Dead end

SCALE

0   250   500 metres

N

BALL'S FALLS TRAIL

LOCATION: Ball's Falls Conservation Area, near Vineland

DISTANCE: 2.5 km/1.5 loop Cataract Trail (Other Area Trails: 1.5 km/0.9 mi. Forest Frolic, 4 km/2.5 mi. linear Twenty Valley Trail)

RATING: Intermediate

HIGHLIGHT: 2 waterfalls, heritage buildings, special events, demonstrations and guided tours

LINK: Jordan Valley/Twenty Valley Trail and Waterfront Trail, Bruce Trail

TRAIL SURFACE: Hard-packed earth, rocks, grass, exposed tree roots.

DIRECTIONS: From the Q.E.W. Niagara, exit 57 at Victoria Avenue (Regional Road 24). Travel south through Vineland to the park entrance at Sixth Avenue. Admission fee applies.

Nestled near two cataracts on the brow of the Escarpment, traces of a 19th-century hamlet at Ball's Falls Historical Park offer historical perspective on the industrial potential near waterways. The Ball Homestead as well as the original 1810 Ball Flour and Grist Mill sit near the Lower Falls.

From the old lime kiln, walk up the escarpment through the arboretum and follow the Bruce Trail near the dugout pond. A set of stairs leads down a steep incline into the broad creek valley where you walk for one kilometre (0.6 mile) passing moss-covered rocks, maidenhair ferns and thick patches of ground hemlock.

Eventually, the Twenty Valley Trail will link Ball's Falls to the village of Jordan with its quaint gift shops and internationally renowned wineries and restaurants. From the creek valley, a stairway will lead to the Jordan Historical Museum of The Twenty, which includes an 1815 log home and schoolhouse.

The Cataract Trail follows the Twenty Mile Creek and leads to both the Upper and Lower Falls.

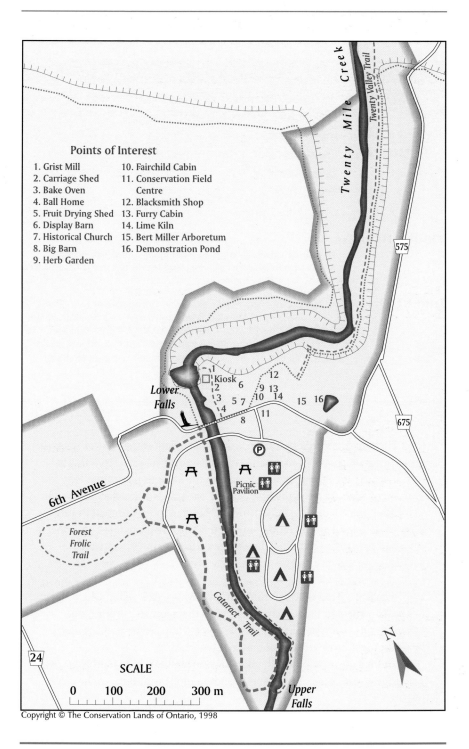

Points of Interest

1. Grist Mill
2. Carriage Shed
3. Bake Oven
4. Ball Home
5. Fruit Drying Shed
6. Display Barn
7. Historical Church
8. Big Barn
9. Herb Garden
10. Fairchild Cabin
11. Conservation Field Centre
12. Blacksmith Shop
13. Furry Cabin
14. Lime Kiln
15. Bert Miller Arboretum
16. Demonstration Pond

Twenty Mile Creek

Twenty Valley Trail

575

675

Kiosk

Lower Falls

6th Avenue

Forest Frolic Trail

Picnic Pavilion

Cataract Trail

Upper Falls

24

N

SCALE

0   100   200   300 m

BEAMER TRAIL

LOCATION:	Beamer Memorial Conservation Area, near Grimsby
DISTANCE:	3 km/1.9 mi. linear (1 km/0.6 mi. linear - wheelchair accessible portion)
RATING:	Intermediate
HIGHLIGHT:	Spring hawk migration, waterfall, Niagara Escarpment
LINK:	Bruce Trail

TRAIL SURFACE:
From Beamer Conservation Area parking lot to the first lookout is stone dust (wheelchair accessible). The rest of the trail is hard-packed earth with tree roots and rocks.

DIRECTIONS: From the Q.E.W. Niagara take exit 71 at Christie Street Exit. Travel south (changes into Mountain Road), turn right on Ridge Rd. W. and right onto Quarrie Rd. You'll see signs for the Conservation Area. To park at Gibson Ave.: from Ridge Rd. W, turn left onto Mountain Rd. and left onto Elm St. At Gibson Ave., turn left and park along the road near the Bruce Trail entrance.

High on the Niagara Escarpment, the open field at the start of the trail is the springtime hot-spot to watch kettles of soaring hawks. From this field, the trail leads into a forest area and heads to the lookout platforms along the escarpment edge. As far as the first lookout, the trail is wheelchair accessible.

From the second lookout, focus your binoculars on Coronation Park below to see a local artist's rendering of a red-tailed hawk painted on a one-and-a-half-metre (five-foot) high limestone surface. From the viewing platforms you'll glance down into the Forty Mile Creek valley and look out over Lake Ontario.

The Bruce Trail descends into the Forty Mile Creek valley, where the trail bears witness to the tenacity of the trees that cling to the limestone rocks. Despite their relatively small size, some white cedars growing along the escarpment brow are several hundred years old.

At the bottom of the trail, walk down the hill to a little footbridge over Forty Mile creek. In October, you may spot salmon swimming up the creek to spawn.

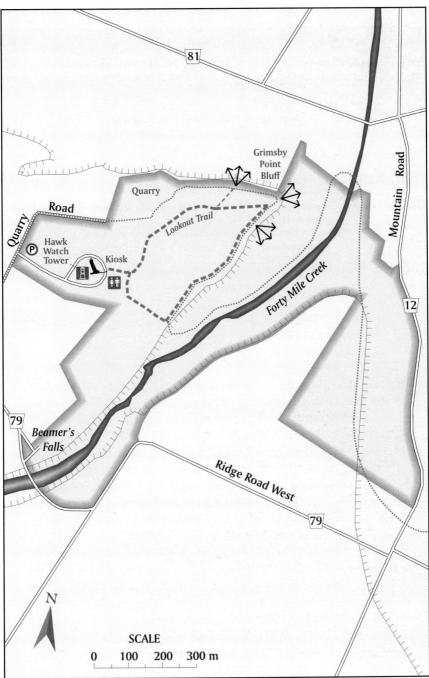

81

Quarry Road

Road

Quarry

Hawk Watch Tower

Ⓟ

Kiosk

Quarry

Grimsby Point Bluff

Lookout Trail

Forty Mile Creek

Mountain Road

12

79

Beamer's Falls

Ridge Road West

79

N

SCALE

0   100   200   300 m

BINBROOK TRAILS

LOCATION: Binbrook Conservation Area, near Binbrook
DISTANCE: 2.3 km/1.4 mi. Lake Niapenco Trail loop
(Other Area Trails: 1 km/0.6 mi. Tyneside Trail
RATING: Beginner
HIGHLIGHT: Migratory waterfowl, wetland flora

TRAIL SURFACE: Gravel, hard-packed earth and grass.

DIRECTIONS: From the Q.E.W. Niagara, exit at Hwy. 20 in Stoney Creek and travel south to Hwy. 56. Drive through Binbrook, turn right on Kirk Road, left on Harrison Road and drive to the park entrance. Gate Admission.

SPECIAL FEATURES: Hunting season.

The shoreline of the 162-hectare (400-acre) Lake Niapenco has pockets of water lilies, swamp loosestrife and water plantain. Osprey dive into the water with talons outstretched for prey and herons wade by the water's edge waiting patiently for fish. Starting through woodlands filled with maple, hickory and ash, the trail periodically dips along the shoreline for a view.

From the open fields, the trail turns a bend and crosses a bridge. With the lake out of sight, the turtles, fish and songbirds are more noticeable. In the summer, when the lake is dotted with colourful windsurf sails, this section is a wonderful retreat. From here, the trail enters the woodlands where quail, pheasants and grouse are frequently spotted.

From the parking lot, a wheelchair-accessible stone dust trail leads to picnic tables, barbecues and a fishing pier all designed for wheelchair access.

The one-kilometre (0.6-mile) Tyneside Trail starts from Tyneside Road and follows the northwest end of the reservoir leading through open field sections, patches of pine forest and meadows of goldenrod and white and purple asters. Along the trail you may glimpse osprey on nesting platforms or mallards in nesting tubes in the water.

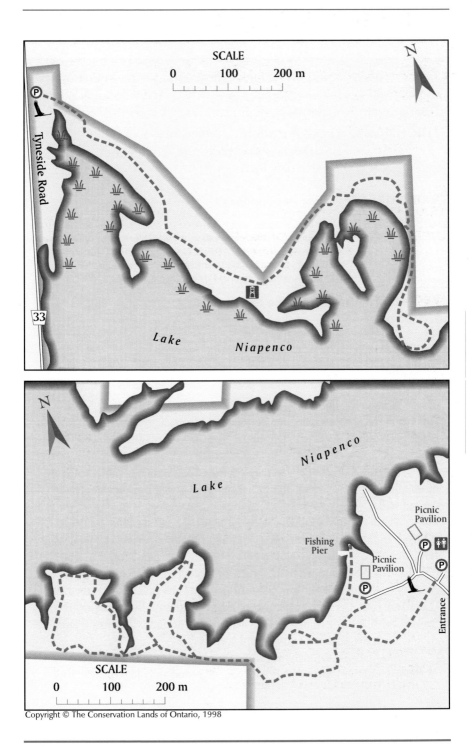

SCALE

0   100   200 m

N

Tyneside Road

33

Lake   Niapenco

N

Lake   Niapenco

Fishing
Pier

Picnic
Pavilion

Picnic
Pavilion

Entrance

SCALE

0   100   200 m

CHIPPAWA CREEK TRAIL

LOCATION: Chippawa Creek Conservation Area, Wellandport
DISTANCE: 2 km/1.2 mi. loop
RATING: Beginner
HIGHLIGHT: Lookout platforms, wheelchair-accessible boardwalk and fishing pier, boat launch

TRAIL SURFACE: Stone dust, boardwalk.

DIRECTIONS: From Q.E.W. Niagara, exit 57 at Victoria Ave. (Regional Rd. 24), travel south past Ball's Falls Conservation Area and turn right onto Hwy. 20. Turn left at Regional Rd. 27 (Bismark) and continue through Wellandport, taking the right fork after crossing the Welland River. Then, turn right on Regional Rd. 45. Admission fee applies.

SPECIAL FEATURES: Hunting season.

Around the 14-hectare (35-acre) Dils Lake, hooded mergansers skim the surface, scooping up floating duckweed and Eurasian Water Milfoil with their bills. Wood ducks with tails in the air search the depths for rooted water lily tubers.

In shallow areas of the wetland, herons wade along the shore, patiently searching for fish to swim within reach; and red-winged blackbirds perch on cattail stalks.

These are the encounters along the leisurely walk at Chippawa Creek Conservation Area, where muskrats scramble in the sedges and children catch largemouth bass and sunfish from lookout platforms. Don't forget to look overhead as sharp-shinned hawks and osprey often soar in search of prey.

Lined with blue vervain, giant thistles and Queen Anne's lace, the Dils Lake Trail is transected by a number of narrow pathways formed by white-tailed deer that drink from its waters early in the morning. The area is also home to red fox, cottontail rabbits and coyotes.

After passing through the campground area, the trail enters open meadows and tree groves replete with oak, dogwood and old farmstead fruit trees.

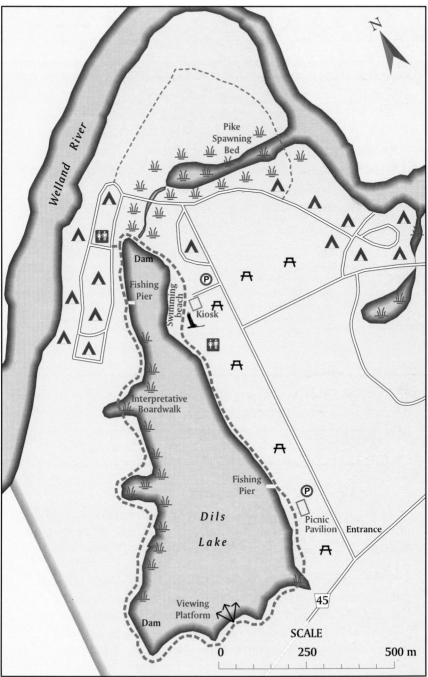

Welland River

Pike
Spawning
Bed

Dam

Fishing
Pier

Swimming Beach

Kiosk

Interpretative
Boardwalk

Dils
Lake

Fishing
Pier

Picnic
Pavilion

Entrance

45

Dam

Viewing
Platform

SCALE

0   250   500 m

N

ST. JOHN'S
SASSAFRAS STROLL

LOCATION:	St. John's Conservation Area, near Fonthill
DISTANCE:	3 km/1.9 mi. loop (Other Area Trails: 0.6 km/0.4 mi. Horseshoe loop, 1.7 km/1.1 mi. St. John's Ridge loop, 1.7/1.1 mi. Tulip Tree loop)
RATING:	Beginner
HIGHLIGHT:	Sassafras tree, Carolinian forest, wheelchair-accessible trail and fishing pier
LINK:	Bruce Trail

TRAIL SURFACE: Hard-packed earth with rocks and grass, boardwalk area.

DIRECTIONS: From the Q.E.W. Niagara, take exit 57 at Victoria Avenue (Regional Rd. #24). Travel south to Hwy. #20 and turn left (east). At Pelham St. in Fonthill, turn north and travel 10 km (this street turns into Hollow Rd.). Near the junction of Barron Rd., there's a small Conservation Area sign on your right.

The sassafras tree, unique to the Carolinian forest, is frequent along this trail. Often referred to as the mitten tree, many of its leaves are three-lobed or mitten-shaped and have a pleasant spicy odour when crushed.

Other Carolinian species, such as the tulip tree, flowering dogwood and butternut also line the trail. A variety of fern species are scattered on the forest floor, including the rough horsetail, the most primitive member of the fern family.

You'll pass a spring-fed pond teeming with water striders and whirligig beetles. This former gravel pit, high in dissolved minerals, has a green algae called chara that grows throughout the pond and stains the water a unique colour.

The forest floor and fallen trees and stumps are covered with mosses, lichens and fungi. Fall is the prime time for mushrooms to appear and hundreds of species have been inventoried in St. John's Conservation Area.

At the end of the trail lies a cold-water trout pond, featuring two wheelchair-accessible fishing piers. At the south end of the pond is a wetland area where dragonflies dart between broad-leaved cattails and sedges.

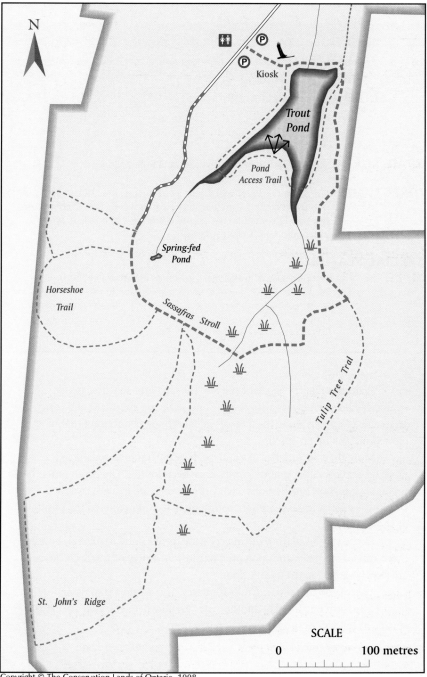

N

Kiosk

Trout
Pond

Pond
Access Trail

Spring-fed
Pond

Horseshoe
Trail

Sassafras Stroll

Tulip Tree Trail

St. John's Ridge

SCALE

0   100 metres

WAINFLEET FOSSIL TRAIL

LOCATION: Wainfleet Wetlands, near Port Colborne
DISTANCE: 1 km/0.6 mi. loop
RATING: Beginner
HIGHLIGHT: Fossil finding

TRAIL SURFACE: Limestone in quarry, grass at Wainfleet Bog.

DIRECTIONS: From The Q.E.W. Niagara, exit 57 at Victoria Ave. (Regional Rd. #24) and travel south. Turn left on Hwy. #3 towards Port Colborne and right on Quarrie Rd. The quarry entrance is at a little gravel indentation 0.6 km on your right.

SPECIAL FEATURES:

Hunting season in Wainfleet Wetlands and Wainfleet Bog.

Wainfleet Quarry is one of the few sites in Ontario where fossils embedded between layers of limestone and shale are abundant and easily accessible. Exposed along the quarry wall and floor, chances are that most pieces you pick up are fossils.

More than 30 varieties of coral, such as the honeycomb-shaped favosites and cone-like solitary corals, have been found. The corals and other organisms, such as brachiopods and crinoids, indicate this area was a tropical sea 380 million years ago, before plate tectonics altered the position of the continent.

Please stay away from the quarry walls as few good fossils can be seen there and falling rocks are a potential hazard. A variety of fossil specimens are clearly visible on the quarry floor.

There is no marked trail in this quarry. You create a trail while wandering from one fossil to another. Be careful where you step during late spring, as killdeer nest right on the quarry floor.

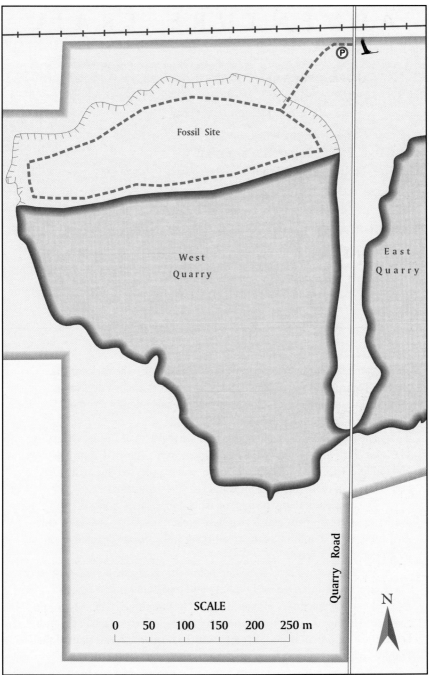

Fossil Site

West
Quarry

East
Quarry

Quarry Road

SCALE

| 0 | 50 | 100 | 150 | 200 | 250 m |

N

WOODEND SILURIAN ADVENTURE TRAIL

LOCATION: Woodend Conservation Area, near Niagara Falls
DISTANCE: 1.6 km/1 mi. linear (Other Area Trails: 11 km/ 6.8 mi. Hardwood Trail)
RATING: Beginner
HIGHLIGHT: Niagara Escarpment
LINK: Bruce Trail

TRAIL SURFACE: Hard-packed earth, rocks and exposed tree roots.

DIRECTIONS: From the Q.E.W. Niagara, exit at Glendale Ave. Travel west to Regional Rd. #70 (Beechwood Road) and turn south. Travel 3 km to the park entrance.

Named after the Silurian geological period when the rocks of the Niagara Escarpment were formed, this trail winds through a deciduous woodlot and meanders along the Escarpment edge, offering views of vineyards and fruit orchards below.

The rock formations along this trail are registers of the area's history. The layers forming the top of the escarpment were deposited approximately 450 million years ago when a shallow, tropical sea covered this area. Coral fossils found in these rocks are indicators of this deposition.

The trail leads along the base of talus slopes, large blocks of overhanging escarpment ledges that have broken off and rolled down cliffs. As for the past 100 million years, weathering and erosion continues as the escarpment slowly retreats.

A red sandstone layer is evident below the escarpment's cap rock layer. These layers were quarried for buildings and represent human activity, evidently taking place here for some time. The remains of a limestone kiln and house foundation erected in the early 1800s are located along the trail below the escarpment edge. This area was the former homestead of United Empire Loyalists and a watch post during the War of 1812.

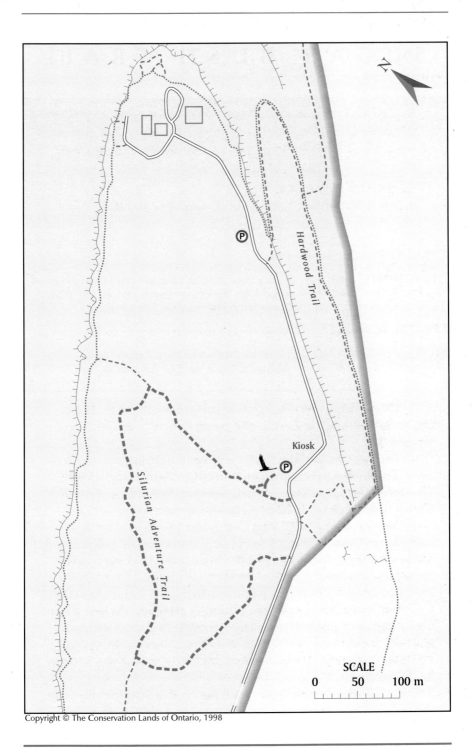

Hardwood Trail

Silurian Adventure Trail

Kiosk

N

SCALE

0   50   100 m

BACKUS WOODS SUGAR BUSH TRAIL

LOCATION: Backus Heritage Conservation Area, Port Rowan
DISTANCE: 6 km/3.7 mi. Sugar Bush Trail loop (Other Area Trails: 3 km/1.9 mi. Floodplain Trail, 6 km/ 3.7 mi. Wetlands Trail)
RATING: Beginner
HIGHLIGHT: Black gum swamp, tulip tree stand, Carolinian Forest

TRAIL SURFACE: Earth and grass.

DIRECTIONS: From Hwy. 403 take Hwy. 24 south (Rest Acres Rd.) through Simcoe. Turn left on Regional Rd. 16, right on Regional Rd. 42 and follow signs for the Conservation Area, north of Port Rowan.

SPECIAL FEATURES: Nature centre and special events.

MORE INFORMATION: (519) 586-2201 Admission fee applies if you use the facilities at Backus Heritage Conservation Area.

The 263 hectares (650 acres) of Backus Woods is one of the largest Carolinian forest tracts in Canada. Old-growth forest encompasses 75% of this land tract.

You'll see Canada's tallest hickory on record and stumps of American sweet chestnut trees, eliminated from most of Canada by a fungal disease. These woodlands are also home to such rarities as the Prothonotary warbler, Eastern Hognose snake and Horace's Duskywing butterfly.

Situated on the Norfolk Sand Plain, Backus Woods has a variety of habitats from beech-sugar maple and black oak upland forests to buttonbush thickets, perennial ponds and spring-flooded swamps of red maple, silver maple and yellow birch.

The straight trunks of the tulip tree, towering five to six metres (19.7 feet) above the forest canopy, impart a feeling of grandeur. The largest tulip trees in Backus, 39 metres (128 feet) tall, are rare in Ontario. A short side trail leads to a black gum swamp with the highest known concentration of this species in Canada. The oldest tree in this stand is estimated to be more than 400 years old.

The three-kilometre (1.9-mile) Flood Plain Trail, starting from the Backus Heritage Conservation Area, connects with the Sugar Bush Trail. Backus Woods has a total of twelve kilometres (7.5 mile) of interconnecting trails.

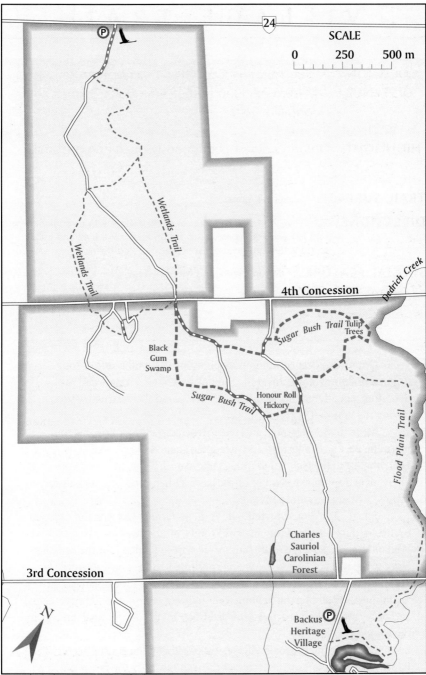

24

SCALE

0   250   500 m

Wetlands Trail

Wetlands Trail

Dedrich Creek

4th Concession

Sugar Bush Trail Tulip Trees

Black Gum Swamp

Sugar Bush Trail

Honour Roll Hickory

Flood Plain Trail

3rd Concession

N

Charles Sauriol Carolinian Forest

Backus Heritage Village

BACKUS HERITAGE VILLAGE TRAIL

LOCATION: Backus Heritage Conservation Area, Port Rowan
DISTANCE: 1 km/0.6 mi. loop (Other Area Trails: 3 km/1.9 mi. Floodplain Trail)
RATING: Beginner
HIGHLIGHT: Ontario's oldest continuously operating grist mill

TRAIL SURFACE: Gravel and grass.

DIRECTIONS: From Hwy. 403 take Hwy. 24 south (Rest Acres Rd.) through Simcoe. Turn left on Regional Rd. 16, right on Regional Rd. 42 and follow signs for the Conservation Area, north of Port Rowan.

SPECIAL FEATURES: Nature centre and special events.

MORE INFORMATION: (519) 586-2201. Admission fee applies.

Ontario's oldest continuously operating grist mill is one of four original buildings along this trail. Built of hand-hewn beams and in operation since 1798, this wooden mill was spared the destructive fires during the War of 1812.

More than 15 restored and reconstructed buildings line this trail. From the Backus Homestead and octagonal-shaped Cherry Valley Schoolhouse to the General Store and Blacksmith Shop, this heritage village offers an extraordinary glimpse of the past. Other structures include log cabins, a cider press and a sawmill.

John C. Backhouse is credited for the well-managed woodlot adjacent to this heritage village. From Backus Woods, lumber was used to rebuild the Welland Canal and large white pines were sent to England for the British Navy's ship masts. Although logging continued on his property until the mid-20th century, John Backhouse pioneered the first forest management techniques. By employing hauling techniques (sleds, skids and horse teams) and only cutting diseased and damaged trees, there was minimal damage in the woodlot.

Upon leaving the main village, walk up the hill to see the Teeterville Baptist Church, built in 1869; stop at the icehouse near the far side of the pond and rest at the picnic tables by the mill race.

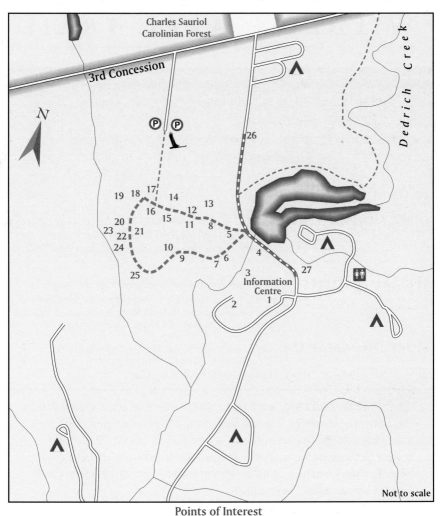

Not to scale

Points of Interest

1. Conservation Education Centre
2. Large Pavilion
3. Small Pavilion
4. John C. Backhouse Mill
5. Garage
6. Museum Building & Backus Gravestones
7. Treadmill, Drag Saw & Stump Puller
8. Driveshed
9. Vittoria Carriage Shop
10. Cider Press
11. Forbes Barn
12. Playhouse
13. Backus Homestead
14. Store fronts of the Heritage Building:
    Aunt Erie's Kitchen
    Dedrick Mercantile
    The Weaving Shop
15. Sawmill
16. Shingle Mill
17. Storage Barn
18. Suderman Barn & Blacksmith Shop
19. Corn Crib
20. Townsend Barn & Farm Implement Driveshed
21. Log House
22. Militia Log House
23. Bake Oven
24. Herb Garden
25. Cherry Valley Schoolhouse
26. Teeterville Baptist Church
27. Ice House

BIG CREEK NATIONAL WILDLIFE AREA TRAIL

LOCATION: Big Creek National Wildlife Area, Long Point
DISTANCE: 2 km/1.2 mi. loop
RATING: Beginner
HIGHLIGHT: Migratory waterfowl, Long Point World Biosphere Reserve

TRAIL SURFACE: Mowed grass.

DIRECTIONS: From Hwy. 403 take Hwy. 24 south (Rest Acres Rd.) through Simcoe. Turn left on Reg. Rd. 16, right on Reg. Rd. 42 and turn south onto Hwy. 59 south. You'll see a sign for Big Creek National Wildlife Area on your right.

SPECIAL FEATURES: During migration period, part of the trail is closed from September 15 to May 15, to not disturb the wildlife. Internationally renowned Long Point Bird Observatory is located five kilometres (3.1 miles) south on Hwy. 59.

MORE INFORMATION: Big Creek National Wildlife Area Headquarters (Environment Canada) (519) 586-2703. Located on Hwy. 59 causeway.

At the base of Long Point, up to 20,000 waterfowl rest and feed in the Big Creek marshes during the peaks of spring and fall migration. Big Creek trail offers a unique opportunity to enter a marsh in this World Biosphere Reserve and Ramsar wetland site. The path enters a diverse marsh habitat, located on the south loop of a dike system used to control water levels and diversify aquatic plant communities.

Cattails, blue-joint and other grasses dominate the outer part of the dike. Growing around the edges of the ponds are waterlilies, bur-reed, swamp loosestrife, wild rice and other important food sources for wildlife. In May and June, you can see numerous amphibians and reptiles such as leopard frogs, eastern fox snakes and blanding's turtles.

More exposed than the rest of the marsh, this area offers a great opportunity to spot common migrants such as mallards, blue-winged teal and wigeon. While standing on the viewing platform, you may regularly observe resident bald eagles or hear the distinctive call of nesting sandhill cranes. The marsh also attracts many shorebirds, terns and marsh birds such as American bitterns, swamp sparrows and marsh wrens. During spring migration, tundra swans travel in flocks of several hundred.

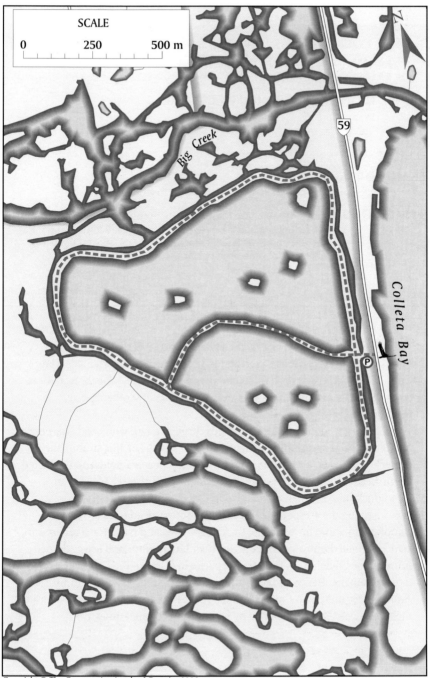

SCALE

0   250   500 m

Big Creek

59

Colleta Bay

P

HAY CREEK TRAIL

LOCATION: Hay Creek Conservation Area, Port Dover
DISTANCE: 2 km/1.2 mi. loop
RATING: Beginner
HIGHLIGHT: Kentucky Coffee Tree

TRAIL SURFACE:
Hard-packed earth, grass, exposed tree roots.

DIRECTIONS: From Hwy. 403, take Hwy. 24 South (Rest Acres Rd.) through Simcoe and continue towards Port Ryerse. Turn left on Radical Rd., right on Ryerse Rd, and you'll see a sign for Hay Creek on your right. The parking lot is south of this sign.

Near the shore of Lake Erie is a 28-hectare (69-acre) woodlot that bursts with life every spring. Surrounded by tobacco and corn fields, Hay Creek exhibits the first dash of colour after a long winter. The forest floor is covered with wood anemones, trilliums, trout lilies and other spring wildflowers.

From the footbridge the trail leads through a red, white and jack pine plantation before reaching a wetland. Along the edge of this swamp, the flowering dogwood's white blossoms, the spring peepers' song and the belted kingfisher's rattle offer more signs of spring. You'll also see blue heron, wood ducks and marsh hawks.

Among the 40 species of trees in this forest, dead trees are left standing as habitat for warblers, flycatchers, owls and bats. You'll also see a stand of small Kentucky Coffee Trees, their large compound leaves draped from coarse branches. A threatened species in Canada, the Kentucky Coffee tree was sought after by pioneers who roasted its seeds as a coffee substitute. Another tree unique to this area is the Pignut Hickory, its name derived from the thick-shelled nuts consumed by hogs during colonial times.

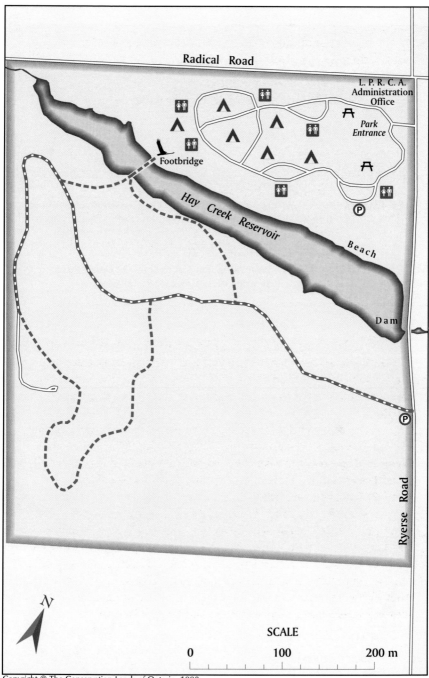

Radical Road

L. P. R. C. A.
Administration
Office

Park
Entrance

Footbridge

Hay Creek Reservoir

Beach

Dam

Ryerse Road

N

SCALE

0   100   200 m

LYNN VALLEY RAIL TRAIL

LOCATION: Simcoe to Port Dover
DISTANCE: 8 km/5 mi. linear
RATING: Beginner
HIGHLIGHT: Historical, river valley

TRAIL SURFACE:
Hard-packed earth and one tire-track areas.

DIRECTIONS: From Hwy. 403, take Hwy. 24 South (Rest Acres Rd.) into Simcoe. Turn left on Woodhouse St. and right on Owen Street to park in Memorial Park. From Hwy. 6 coming into Port Dover from Hamilton, turn right on Mill Rd. or Queen St.

MORE INFORMATION: Lynn Valley Trail Association, 137 Decou Road, Simcoe ON N3Y 4K2 (519) 428-3292.

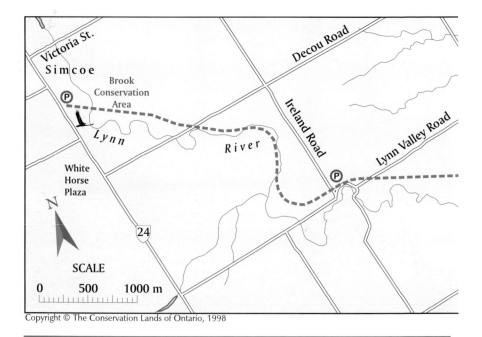

This former railway line was established along the Pioneer River trail in 1873. The trail crosses four trestle bridges, passes Carolinian forest vegetation and follows historic aboriginal and pioneer travel routes. Interspersed between river crossings are wild raspberry, blackberry and strawberry patches, providing welcome breaks on a hot summer day.

This pathway follows the Lynn River from Simcoe to Port Dover, the only road travel, a 120-metre (394-foot) section along Lynn Valley Road. There is an option to lengthen the trail and cycle down Port Dover's Main St. to the marina and harbour shops.

It was the Neutral Indians who first traveled the creek valleys in the fall to catch and dry whitefish, returning with them to their inland villages. In the mid 1790s, settlers travelling from Port Dover traversed the valley, then known as Patterson's Creek. Some established mills and foundries, remnants of which still exist. If you take a side trip to Brook Conservation Area, the Brook Woollen Mill is still visible.

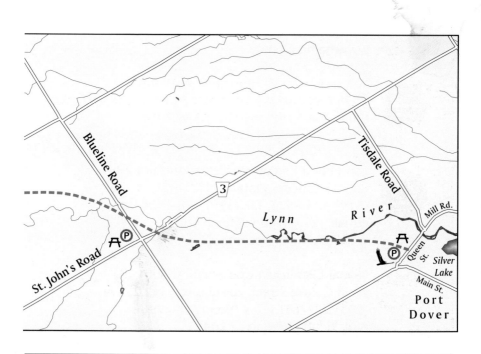

REFERENCES

 THE CONSERVATION LANDS OF ONTARIO
400 Clyde Rd., P.O. Box 729
Cambridge, Ontario N1R 5W6
1-888-376-2212, fax (519) 621-4844
e-mail: conservationlands@grandriver.on.ca
www.conservationlands.com

CONSERVATION AUTHORITIES

 Grand River Conservation Authority
400 Clyde Rd., Box 729, Cambridge, ON N1R 5W6
(519) 621-2761, fax (519) 621-4844
e-mail: postmaster@grandriver.on.ca
website:www.grandriver.on.ca

 Hamilton Region Conservation Authority
838 Mineral Springs Rd., P.O. Box 7099
Ancaster, ON L9G 3L3
1-888-319-HRCA, fax (905) 648-4622
e-mail: nature@hamrca.on.ca, website:
www.hamrca.on.ca

 Halton Region Conservation Authority
2596 Britannia Rd. W., R.R. #2 Milton, ON L9T 2X6
(905) 336-1158, fax (905) 336-7014
e-mail: admin@hrca.on.ca, website: www.hrca.on.ca

 Long Point Region Conservation Authority
R.R. #3 Simcoe, Ontario N3Y 4K2
(519) 428-4623, fax (519) 428-1520,
e-mail: conservation@lprca.on.ca
website: www.lprca.on.ca

 Niagara Peninsula Conservation Authority
2358 Centre Street, Allanburg, ON L0S 1A0
(905) 227-1013, fax (905) 227-2998
e-mail: NPCA@niagara.com
website: www.conservation-niagara.on.ca

TRIP PLANNING

The Conservation Lands of Ontario program has a number of partners. The following pages outline a few of the services, accommodations and outlets available near trails featured in this book. Phone the Conservation Lands of Ontario hotline (1-888-376-2212) for a complete list and help with your trip planning needs. Hot link to our members through our website – www.conservationlands.com.

GRAND RIVER
CONSERVATION AUTHORITY CAMPSITES

Brant, Brantford, (519) 752-2040
130 serviced sites, 270 unserviced

Byng Island, Dunnville
(905) 774-5755
109 serviced sites, 225 unserviced

Conestogo Lake, Elmira
(519) 638-2873
70 serviced sites, 134 unserviced

Elora Gorge, Elora, (519) 846-9742
250 serviced sites, 300 unserviced

Guelph Lake, Guelph, (519) 824-5061
104 serviced sites, 190 unserviced

Laurel Creek, Waterloo,
(519) 884-6620
68 serviced sites, 58 unserviced

Pinehurst Lake, Cambridge
(519) 442-4721
175 serviced sites, 125 unserviced

Rockwood, Guelph, (519) 856-9543
46 serviced sites, 53 unserviced

LONG POINT REGION
CONSERVATION AUTHORITY CAMPSITES

Haldimand, Selkirk, (905) 776-2700
183 serviced sites, 47 unserviced

Hay Creek, Simcoe, (519) 428-4622
45 unserviced sites

Norfolk, Simcoe, (519) 428-1460
160 serviced sites, 25 unserviced

Inland Outfitters and Izzy's Eatery, Waterford,
(519) 443-4702
100 unserviced sites
Little Lake, Otterville, (519) 446-2362

30 serviced sites, 15 unserviced

Backus Heritage, Port Rowan, (519) 586-2201
60 serviced sites, 90 unserviced

Deer Creek, Langton, (519) 875-2874
40 unserviced sites

NIAGARA PENINSULA
CONSERVATION AUTHORITY CAMPSITES

Long Beach, Wainfleet, (905) 899-3462
110 serviced sites, 165 unserviced

Chippawa Creek, Wellandport, (905) 386-6387
60 serviced sites, 40 unserviced

ACCOMMODATION

Bluebird Meadow Bed and Breakfast, Gadshill, (519) 656-2731
Enjoy comfortable, country hospitality. Observe nature in our wetland habitats. Walk, birdwatch, relax and enjoy!

Cedarbrook Farm, Puslinch, (905) 659-1566
Elegant Victorian Farmhouse & Coachhouse on secluded 40 hectares (100 acres). Individual or corporate.

Elora Mill Restaurant and Inn, Elora, (519) 846-5356
Fine dining and accommodation in a unique country setting.

Langdon Hall, Cambridge, (519) 740-2100
One of the most elegant country inns in Canada.

Tintern Vacation Bed and Breakfast, Vineland, (905) 563-4000
Country charm in the heart of Niagara's Wine Country. Overlooks Twenty Mile Creek.

Venture Inn Burlington-on-the-Lake, Burlington, (905) 681-0762
Country warmth in the heart of downtown Burlington, picturesquely situated on the shores of Lake Ontario.

ADVENTURE PLANNERS

Equinox Adventures, Willowdale, (416) 222-2223
Rock climbing, whitewater kayaking and canoeing, advance rescue techniques.

Higher Ground, Guelph, (519) 823-8088
Rock Climbing and Learning Program Centres. Adventure based, team building and outdoor experiential learning programs.

ATTRACTIONS

Cave Springs Cellars, Jordan, (905) 562-3581
Growers and Vintners of Fine Wine

Haldimand House, Caledonia 1-800 897-1190
Purveyors of Fine Gifts and Gourmet Shoppe

Halton Region Museum, Milton, (905) 875-2200
Combine an escarpment adventure with exploring Halton's fascinating history.

Henry of Pelham Family Estate, St. Catharines, (905) 684-8423
Henry of Pelham family estate is the leading edge in VQA Wines.

Hernder Estate Wines, St. Catharines, (905) 684-3300
Wine Lover's Paradise - Hernder Estate Wines

Kernal Peanuts Ltd., Vittoria, (519) 426-9222
Nuttin' But the Best! Gift shop, pre-arranged factory tours available.

Norfolk Estate Winery, St. Williams, (519) 586-2237
Ontario's First Gold Medal Winning Apple Based Winery. "Taste the Difference for Yourself."

Pinetree Native Centre of Brant/ "Kanata", Brantford, (519) 752-5132

Rainey Ginseng Farms Ltd., Waterford, (519) 443-5931
Tour the farm and choose from a wide variety of our ginseng products.

Royal Botanical Gardens, Burlington, (905) 527-1158
Paradise Found - 1100 hectares (2700 acres) of gardens, forests, wetlands, wildlife and trails.

Ruthven Park, Cayuga, (905) 772-0560
A treasured National Site, rich in natural, historical, architectural and agricultural significance.

Sweet Grass Gardens, Hagersville, (519) 445-4828
Specializing in the preservation of plant species indigenous to North America.

The Arboretum, Guelph, (519) 824-4120 ext 2113
Plant collections, gardens, forests and meadows in an extensive greenspace.

The Herbal Touch, Otterville, (519) 879-6812
Herbs, plants, wreaths, baskets and lectures.

Vineland Estate Winery Ltd., Vineland, (905) 562-7088
"Ontario's most picturesque winery" offers lunch and dinner seven days a week, all year.

Wellington County Museum, Fergus, (519) 846-0916
National Historic Site, historical exhibits, art shows, festivals, gardens and trails.

Woodland Cultural Centre, Brantford, (519) 759-2650
Take a journey back in time with Canada's First Nations and experience a whole new world.

INFORMATION

Cambridge Vistor & Convention Bureau, Cambridge, (519) 653-1424
Call us for information on beautiful and exciting Cambridge!

Fergus District Chamber of Commerce, Fergus, (519) 843-5140
Experience rich Scottish heritage, limestone buildings, parks, shops and gardens.

The Village of Elora (Chamber of Commerce), Elora, (519) 846-9841
Gorges, galleries and more! Call for information about our charming village.

The Hike Ontario Guide To Walks Through Carolinian Ontario
by Brad Cundiff (Hike Ontario 1-800-422-0552)

OUTFITTERS

Blue Heron Raft Company, Brantford, (519) 754-0145
Come take a float through history!

Cycle Ontario Experience, Kitchener, (519) 653-8582
Experience Ontario in a unique way, wrapped up in one great package ready for you to enjoy.

Grand Experiences, Paris, (519) 442-3654
Come with us for a mini vacation and experience the view from our backyard.

The Grand River Canoe Company, Brantford, (519) 759-0040
Canoes, kayaks, shuttle service, bikes. Relax, enjoy, food, sun, experience it!

Grand River Troutfitters, Fergus, (519) 787-4359
Ontario's Flyfishing Education Centre, Guiding & Full Service Authorized Orvis Retail Store.

Grindstone Angling and Specialties, Waterdown, (905) 689-0880
Your one-stop fly-fishing shop in Ontario. We will help you plan a truly enjoyable fishing adventure.

Horseback Adventures by Martin's Farm Products - Waterloo, (519) 888-6503
Ride a Tennessee Walking Horse along the Conestoga and Grand Rivers.

Milestone Stables, Campbellville, (905) 854-0762
Horseback riding on the Niagara Escarpment.

Two Rivers Canoe, Paris, (519) 442-2415
2 & 5 hour canoe trips on the Grand and Nith Rivers. Shuttle service included.

RESTAURANTS

Dakota's Waterfront Cafe, Burlington, (905) 632-6544
Chef's Adventures - everyday is a new adventure, always fresh food, innovative and most inviting.

Morgans on the Grand, Paris, (519) 442-5313
Traditional Ale House with riverside deck and casual atmosphere.

The Country Kitchen, Port Rowan, (519) 586-7172
Home Cookin' at its Best!

TOUR OPERATORS

C.S. Powell Charters Ltd., Simcoe, (519) 426-1414
Tours and charters. Lake Erie, Port Dover and Long Point Bay from a unique perspective.

Down To Earth, Dundas, (905) 627-3140
Specialists in year-round outdoor, interactive and interpretive programs.

Grand Voyageur Tours, Dunnville, (905) 774-6900
Journey through the Grand River delta in an authentic Voyageur canoe and learn about the history of a river.

Green Planet Tour Company, Hamilton, (905) 540-1441
Specializing in nature viewing, Niagara Escarpment waterfalls, Carolinian Forest tours.

Real McCoy Charters and Tours, Troy, (905) 777-0873
Providers of transportation with 16, 20, 47 and 56 seat capacity. Complete package tours arranged.

Robin Hood Tours, Goderich, (519) 524-4540
Travel specialists. Air, Cruise, Motorcoach.

Steve Bauer Bike Tours Inc., Vineland, (905) 562-0788
Specializing in quality bike tours for different fitness levels and interests.

Wyldewood Llama Treks, Freelton, (905) 659-1413
Organized group hikes with eco-friendly llamas.

INDEX

ALPHABETICAL TRAILS LISTING

TRAIL LISTING BY COMMUNITY

Trail Features at a Glance

G - Group Camping   A - All Terrain Wheelchairs Available

GRAND RIVER CONSERVATION AUTHORITY

Trail	Page #
Apps' Mill Nature Trail (Brantford)	16
Cambridge to Paris Rail Trail (Cambridge and Paris)	18
Elora Gorge Trail (Elora)	20
Elora Cataract Trailway (Elora and Cataract)	22
F.W.R. Dickson Trail (Cambridge)	24
Luther Marsh Trail (Orangeville)	26
Pinehurst Lake Trail (Cambridge)	28
Rockwood Trail (Rockwood)	30
Shade's Mills Trail (Cambridge)	32

HALTON REGION CONSERVATION AUTHORITY

Trail	Page #
Crawford Lake Trail (Milton)	34
Iroquoian Village Trail (Milton)	36
Hilton Falls Trail (Milton)	38
Kelso/Glen Eden Trail (Milton)	40
Mountsberg Trail (Campbellville)	42
Raptor Centre Trail (Campbellville)	44
Mount Nemo Trail (Burlington)	46
Rattlesnake Point Trail (Milton)	48

Feature matrix (columns are trail page numbers):

Feature	16	18	20	22	24	26	28	30	32	34	36	38	40	42	44	46	48
Fossils/Geology			•					•		•		•	•			•	•
Grand River		•	•	•													
Carolinian Forest	•	•					•			•					•	•	•
Niagara Escarpment										•	•	•	•			•	•
Birding	•	•	•	•	•	•	•	•	•	•		•	•	•	•	•	•
Special Events	•									•	•		•	•	•		
Interpretive/Natural Centre	•									•	•		•	•	•		
Heritage Site	•	•		•			•			•	•	•	•	•			
Camping			•				•	•					•G			•G	
Handicapped Access		•								•A	•A		•A	•A			
Group Trail Bookings	•	•	•	•		•	•		•	•	•	•	•	•	•		
Viewing Area		•	•		•	•		•		•		•	•	•		•	•
Horseback Riding											•						
Cross Country Skiing	•		•	•			•			•		•		•	•		•
Cycling	•			•								•	•				

102

Table of trail features (features listed across; trails listed down). A "•" indicates the feature applies to that trail.

Trail	Page #	Fossils/Geology	Grand River	Carolinian Forest	Niagara Escarpment	Birding	Special Events	Interpretive/Natural Centre	Heritage Site	Camping	Handicapped Access	Group Trail Bookings	Viewing Area	Horseback Riding	Cross Country Skiing	Cycling
HAMILTON REGION CONSERVATION AUTHORITY																
Christie 'Round-the-Lake Trail (Flamborough)	50			•	•	•	•					•			•	•
Crooks' Hollow Historical Trail (Flamborough)	52			•	•				•							
Dundas Valley Trails (Ancaster)	54	•		•	•	•	•	•	•		•A	•	•	•	•	
Hamilton to Brantford Rail Trail (Hamilton and Brantford)	56			•	•	•		•			•			•		•
Red Hill Valley Recreational Trail (Hamilton)	58			•	•	•	•									•
Royal Botanical Gardens North Shore Trail (Hamilton)	60			•	•	•	•			•		•	•			
Spencer Gorge Waterfalls Trail (Flamborough)	62	•		•	•	•		•				•	•			
Valens Boardwalk Trail (Flamborough)	64			•	•	•	•				•	•	•		•	
Westfield Heritage Trail (Rockton)	66						•		•			•				
Westfield Woods Trail (Rockton)	68					•	•		•			•		•	•	
NIAGARA PENINSULA CONSERVATION AUTHORITY																
Ball's Falls Trail (near Vineland)	70	•		•	•	•	•		•			•	•		•	
Beamer Trail (near Grimsby)	72	•		•	•	•	•				•	•	•		•	
Binbrook Trails (near Binbrook)	74					•					•	•	•		•	
Chippawa Creek Trail (Wellandport)	76					•					•	•	•		•	
St. John's Sassafras Stroll (near Fonthill)	78			•		•	•			•	•					
Wainfleet Fossil Trail (near Port Colborne)	80	•		•		•	•						•		•	
Woodend Silurian Adventure Trail (near Niagara Falls)	82	•			•	•						•	•		•	

	Backus Woods Sugar Bush Trail (Port Rowan)	Backus Heritage Village Trail (Port Rowan)	Big Creek National Wildlife Area Trail (Long Point)	Hay Creek Trail (Port Dover)	Lynn Valley Rail Trail (Simcoe and Port Dover)
Page #	84	86	88	90	92
Fossils/Geology					
Grand River					
Carolinian Forest	•			•	•
Niagara Escarpment					
Birding	•		•	•	•
Special Events	•	•		•	•
Interpretive/ Natural Centre	•	•			
Heritage Site		•			
Camping		•		•	
Handicapped Access		•			
Group Trail Bookings	•	•		•	•
Viewing Area			•		•
Horseback Riding					•
Cross Country Skiing	•			•	•
Cycling	•			•	•

LONG POINT REGION CONSERVATION AUTHORITY